Manager's Guide to
Social Media

Other titles in the Briefcase Books series include:

To learn more about titles in the Briefcase Books series go to
www.briefcasebooks.com

Manager's Guide to Social Media

Scott Klososky

McGraw-Hill

New York Chicago San Francisco Lisbon
London Madrid Mexico City Milan New Delhi
San Juan Seoul Singapore Sydney Toronto

The McGraw·Hill Companies

Copyright © 2011 by The McGraw-Hill Companies, Inc. All rights reserved. Printed in the United States of America. Except as permitted under the United States Copyright Act of 1976, no part of this publication may be reproduced or distributed in any form or by any means, or stored in a data base or retrieval system, without the prior written permission of the publisher.

1 2 3 4 5 6 7 8 9 0 DOC/DOC 1 9 8 7 6 5 4 3 2 1 0

ISBN   978-0-07-175433-0
MHID   0-07-175433-4

This is a CWL Publishing Enterprises book developed for McGraw-Hill by CWL Publishing Enterprises, Inc., Madison, Wisconin, www.cwlpub.com.

Library of Congress Cataloging-in-Publication Data

Klososky, Scott.
  Manager's guide to social media / by Scott Klososky
     p. cm.
  Includes index
  ISBN 978-0-07-175433-0 (alk. paper)
  1. Personal Internet use in the workplace. 2. Social media. 3. Information technology—Management. 4. Management—Social aspects. I. Title.
  HF5549.5.P39K 2011
  006.7024'65—dc 22

                                                          2010039597

McGraw-Hill books are available at special quantity discounts to use as premiums and sales promotions, or for use in corporate training programs. For more information, please write to the Director of Special Sales, McGraw-Hill Professional, Two Penn Plaza, New York, NY 10121-2298. Or contact your local bookstore.

This book is printed on acid-free paper.

Contents

Introduction

Rarely does a new set of tools come along—seemingly rising out of nowhere—and become such a powerful way to get business done. At the same time, while social technology tools are indispensible to some people, others can't grasp what they are or why they matter. In just the last few years Web sites like Facebook, MySpace, YouTube, and Flickr have become commonly used by hundreds of millions of people. Services like Twitter, RSS feeds, blogs, and LinkedIn connect us in real time to the thoughts and lives of thousands of people at once so that we can assemble rivers of information in ways we simply never had before. All of these new capabilities have the potential to improve our quality of life and our productivity at work. Of course, therein lies a manager's dilemma!

There's clearly huge potential for social tools to help organizations reach goals and prosper. There can also be great challenges because the same tools that connect organizations with their customers and clients also connect workers with all their friends. The same tools that help organizations create content and distribute it for free to millions of people also allow employees to access any type of content at their desk at work. At this moment you either agree that these tools are a powerful element for the good, or you might believe that they're the worst things to hit the workforce since the company holiday party. Regardless of where you stand on social tech, we all must face the fact that it's here to stay, and it's just a baby at this point. There will be more capabilities to come and billions more people who will join the ranks and use these tools over the coming years.

Navigating our new socially infused world isn't a simple thing for managers. There are so many rules that haven't yet been put in place, and we haven't had time to develop social mores of what is acceptable. Social technologies have the power to impact every area of an organization. We haven't yet figured out how to harness this power and head it in the right direction. In many cases, people don't even understand what social technologies are and all of the concepts and uses that come under this banner description!

We wrote this book to serve as one of the first how-to guides for managing the people who are now bringing these tools to work and are tasked with figuring out how to leverage them. The rewards for getting this right will be huge; the penalties for mismanaging a corporate culture now adopting these tools (whether you like it or not) could be unfortunate. We'll teach you what social technology is and then provide information about how to put it into productive practice.

Chapter Highlights

The workplace has never been faced with a set of new tools whose use is growing so rapidly. Add to that they really can't easily be controlled. Workers can now participate in any type of social site through their mobile devices, meaning they don't need your equipment to connect with the world. With many people on salary and working flex hours, there's not a distinct line between work time and nonwork time, especially when people are investing time to keep their personal contacts fresh in order to get work done. What might appear as wasting time to one manager could be recognized as valuable investments being made by an employee in nurturing his or her network to another. There are solutions to all this complexity, and we'll make the world of social tech simpler for you—and that's a promise!

Throughout this book, we've taken care to both explain the new issues that social technologies are creating, as well as the wonderful benefits of its use. In some cases, we suggest ideas that could help you be a star on your team. In other cases, we share best practices we're seeing in organizations that are leading their competition with the use of social tools. For example, we highlight the following areas:

■ What social technologies are and why they're important

■ How organizations can fit social tech into their strategies in a healthy way

■ The importance of managing the use of social tech as a tool, and the dangers of allowing it to happen organically

■ How to choose the best social tools for your organization, and how to stay current in a world where new tools come out every day

■ How to integrate social technologies into your sales model

■ The importance of managing your online reputation (you being the organization and the management)

■ How to build powerful rivers of information using social technologies and simultaneously raise the organizational IQ

■ How to administer the socially delivered organizational voice

■ The benefits of measuring and analyzing the use of social tech, especially return on investment

■ The best practices for implementing social tools with velocity, and how you can use them in ways that'll create value for any organization

■ The future of social tech, including where it's likely to go and why

Because social technologies are so new and becoming such a difference-maker in achieving goals inside organizations, there's huge potential for you to take the information in this book and apply it in ways that advance your career. Don't miss the opportunity to get in front of this movement and be a leader the rest of the managers will look to for the best practices in the use of social tools. We'd love to play that role for you.

We hope you'll be able to refer to this book as a step-by-step guide for years to come, and also that you'll pull out a handful of ideas and be the evangelist in the organization for getting them institutionalized. Now's the time to grab this powerful trend and use it to help reach your company's goals!

Special Features

The idea behind the books in the Briefcase series is to give you practical information written in a friendly person-to-person style. The chapters are short, deal with tactical issues, and include lots of examples. They also feature numerous boxes designed to give you different types of specific information. Here's more information about the boxes you'll find in this book.

KEY TERM

Every subject has some special jargon, especially one like social technology. These boxes provide explanations and insights into ideas and terms.

SMART

MANAGING

These boxes give you tips and tactics for using the ideas in this book to intelligently take advantage of social technology tools to manage your team and organization.

These boxes give you how-to and insider hints on techniques savvy professionals use to successfully implement social technology in your organization.

It's always useful to have examples that show how the idea and techniques in the book are applied. These boxes appear frequently throughout and explain how real companies use social technology.

These boxes warn you where things could go wrong when you're planning and implementing social technology in your organization and what to do about it.

How can you be sure you won't make a mistake when you're implementing the techniques the book describes? You can't, but these boxes give you practial advice on how to minimize the possibility of an error.

TOOLS

Social media and the technology behind it are tools for communicating and connecting with employees, customers, and all the stakeholders in the organization. These boxes call attention to special items you should know about.

Social Technologies: An Introduction

K im runs a marketing office with six direct reports. Four of her people are under 32 years old and have been with the company for less than two years. More and more, she observes them spending time on their computers using Facebook, Twitter, and watching YouTube videos. She can't help noticing that they send links to each other and share interesting articles and videos. At times she's sure they're helping to expose each other to new ideas and information, yet she also suspects they use company time to communicate with friends. Increasingly, her four young direct reports spend time on their mobile devices during meetings, either texting, checking social sites, or taking notes; it's hard to say.

Their performance still seems to be up to par, but Kim wonders if they could do a better job if all these online tools, to which they seem to be addicted, didn't distract them. In the last six months she's noticed that they're putting in less hours at the office, yet they also seem to be working after hours and sometimes on weekends. Worst of all, they seem to have command of new tools that are regular parts of their day, and Kim has never heard of most of them. Part of her wants to encourage them to quit spending so much time online, and the other part senses this is a new way of working that can be effective. What should she do next?

Managing people is always a challenging task. Human beings can be unpredictable, emotional, and hard to organize into a frictionless team, even for the best leader. Add to this mixture sophisticated technology tools that enable them to communicate for free with millions of people instantly, anywhere in the world, and you have the recipe for disaster—or stunningly good results. Today's organizations have never had four generations that are more different in how they view the world and have never seen a fire hose full of free tools coming at them like we see from the Web today.

These dynamics offer managers a wonderful opportunity to impact the way social technologies get integrated into the organization's daily activities. On the other side of this wonderful opportunity is the possibility of a tremendous mess if managers are uneducated about or don't understand these technologies.

If managers fail to provide a good example by using these tools personally, they won't only be failing as leaders, they'll also create a chasm between themselves and those they lead. It's now clear that social technologies aren't a fad, and they're here to stay. This demands that managers become knowledgeable about the field.

A Bit of History

Without huge fanfare, the term *Web 2.0* made its debut shortly after the dotcom crash of 2001. People were searching for an answer to the question of where the Web would go after its overheated rise in the late '90s, and subsequent return to earth. While some people wrote off the Internet as having much less impact than was predicted, the first signs of a new era were appearing. Instead of people just connecting with companies offering products, they began to connect with each other.

Communities of interest began to form where people from around the world with specific areas of commonality could find each other and share information, ideas, opinions, and files. Then savvy, young entrepreneurs began to build tools that let us share content and opinions in various formats—for free. Whereas Web 1.0 is all about e-commerce, Web 2.0 is about *connection*. So much so, that the term Web 2.0 gave way to a more specific moniker: *social technologies*.

The Vocabulary

There seems to be confusion around the vocabulary of social relevancy, social media, social networking, and social technologies, so let's clear that up first. *Social technologies* is the umbrella term that encompasses three discreet areas of the Web 2.0 era. There is actually a fourth catchall

> **Social Technologies**
> Denotes all areas of the social sphere on the Web. When people use the incorrect vocabulary to describe an area of the social sphere, they confuse and weaken the ability to discern the three areas: social relevancy, social media, and social networking. Once you understand the difference among these three areas, you're better prepared to manage people to successfully use them.
>
> **KEY TERM**

category that I will just say encompasses all of the discreet tasks that people are putting the word "social" in front of, for example, social CRM and social recruiting. For our purposes, it's important that you understand the three major categories so you can invest resources into being productive with all of them.

Social Relevancy

The first is *social relevancy*. This describes the concept of an online reputation or credentials, and all the tools available in this area. These include the online reputations of an organization and an individual. Both have a level of social relevancy online today—whether they choose to influence it or not. Think of social relevancy as your online credentials. When a potential customer, partner, vendor, or investor looks online to learn about your organization, the collection of links, user opinions, and content they can access adds up to your online relevancy. At an individual level, when HR departments, buyers, partners, or potential girlfriends or boyfriends search for you online, they'll also find content, opinions, and links that will comprise your online credentials.

Social Media

The second is *social media*. This describes any Web site or service that facilitates using a piece of media to share an idea, advertise, promote, or deliver content. Media in this sense could be documents (scribd.com), presentations (slideshare.com), photos (flickr.com), or videos (youtube.com.) For some reason, the media (newpapers, TV, radio) seem to use this term often as the umbrella term, and that just confuses the matter. Social media is already a powerful source of information transmission on a worldwide scale. People with an expertise in a discreet area or with something important to get across are leveraging social media sites to "talk to" 1.8 billion other people—for free.

Social Networking

The third part of social technologies is *social networking*. This describes any Web site or service that facilitates people communicating one-to-one, or one-to-many, in a conversation. This includes MySpace, Facebook, Ning, LinkedIn, Plaxo, Twitter, Foursquare, blogging, etc. Social networking includes everything from eCommunities to broadcasting communications through text, audio, or video in a live format. Social networking is about connection through conversation among people independently or through organizations speaking with an organizational voice.

There is actually a catchall category that should be mentioned, and that is all the "socially augmented" services that are now being identified by putting the word "social" in front of the activity. For example, social CRM (customer relationship management) and social recruiting, just to name a couple. It's likely that for the next decade we will attach the "social" moniker to many tasks and will eventually just drop the need to specify that people are using social tools to augment the task.

Describing What Social Tech Really Is . . .

There seem to be many people—especially in the older generations—who struggle to understand the whole phenomenon of social tech. It can seem like a dangerous place where privacy is thrown out the window and security does not exist. They cringe when they see a teenager texting at the dinner table. They have little idea why someone would watch YouTube as if it were a TV channel, and they clearly are confused by the concept of Twitter and why people would share their thoughts and activities with the world five times a day. Social tech feels like an amorphous trend that is growing quickly, in lots of directions, with no instruction manuals.

We can define this pretty easily if you think of social technologies as a *collection of new forms of communication and community.*

DESCRIBING SOCIAL TECH TO OTHERS SMART

Once you become known as a manager who gets what social tech is, you'll find yourself having to describe it to people who are struggling to grasp the concept. A good piece of advice is to keep it simple and just get across that it's a set of tools that help people MANAGING communicate in new ways over the Web. Just explain that the only difference between Twitter, Facebook, and the cell phone is each provides a unique aspect for communicating in a specific way, at a specific time. For example, Twitter is real-time stream communication, Facebook is community-based communication with a group of your choosing, and the cell phone is audio communication that is typically point-to-point.

With the Internet acting as a transport service, hundreds of Web tools are being built (and offered for free in most cases) that provide various ways to connect with others. These connections can be with people we know personally, or collections of people who share our interests. They often provide information streams in real time, meaning that, for example, information about an event is shared as it happens or that someone has a thought to share and puts it out there. Along the way, we have also developed ways to search and find individuals, and to connect to them in ways based on the information stream we prefer to receive or provide.

These tools aren't restricted to a chosen few. They're offered to anyone with Web access, and that number is growing by millions of people a month. This is an amazing thing because never before in human history have we had the ability to talk to nearly two billion people in a free and unfiltered manner. Not only that, there's a growing list of possible ways we can "talk" to the rest of the world. We can communicate through mobile devices by texting and e-mail, with pictures, videos, in 140-character microblogs, and with full-sized blogs.

We can use free tools to call someone anywhere in the world, and oh, by the way, you can add a video to a call as well (Skype). The scale and speed of our newfound ability to communicate with each other is staggering.

With every blessing comes a curse. For people who manage others, this newfound capability adds to an already-growing list of complex areas that need supervision. This isn't a collection of new tools to ignore, block, or for-

> **KEY TERMS**
>
> **Microblogging** Refers to any service that delivers a message to a person, or group of people, in a restricted number of characters. The "micro" prefix indicates that this message is typically fewer than 200 characters (for Twitter that number is 140). The "blogging" distinguishes the exercise from text messaging in that it's designed to deliver the message to many people and, in some cases, even to millions of people with the press of a button.
>
> **Blocking and Monitoring** Whenever we use the terms "blocking usage" or "monitoring usage," we are referring to the ability to set a firewall in the data center to literally deny the usage of a Web site. It's possible to block all sites that use video, or just one site at a time if it's felt that usage of the site would be abused or is inappropriate at the office.
>
> Monitoring refers to the practice of logging the amount of time spent on a site, and what sites an employee has visited from his or her work computer.

bid. Too many people rely on them in their personal lives and to enhance their business careers, especially the younger generations who have adopted these tools quickly and fearlessly.

Understand this: social tech is more than Facebook, LinkedIn, and Twitter. From an organizational standpoint, these applications are a tiny part of the overall picture. We explain in detail many of the concepts that now fall under the social tech umbrella. By the end of this book, you'll have a broader vision of how pervasive this new field will become. Hence, leaders need to develop management skills to leverage social tools instead of being frustrated by them.

How Did We Get Here?

Before we discuss best practices for managing how people can use social technologies to enhance performance, let's step back and examine why social tech is exploding at all. Nothing like this happens without a reason behind what drives the heavy adoption of a tool.

Understanding these dynamics can help us envision where it might go. It's an interesting scenario we find ourselves in. The youngest people in the workforce have naturally adapted to many of the new social tools, while the oldest generation only picks it up after its clear value has been proven.

The Drivers of Usage

When viewed from a high level, what drives social media and social networking is people's basic desire to connect and communicate, which for most of history has been limited by geography. As transportation improved in the twentieth century we were able to expand our reach in communicating and connecting. For that entire century, we used the telephone as a connection device that could electronically allow us to reach out and "touch" someone. Just as new inventions like the telephone and the automobile changed our lives in dramatic ways at the beginning of the last century, social tech is changing our lives in this century. It's all about connection and communication—plain and simple.

This Is Nothing New

Social tech has not created a new human dynamic; it simply has enhanced our ability to communicate with others—anywhere, anytime, in multiple ways, and usually for free. It also has allowed us to build communities of interest that don't concern themselves with demographics, geography, or language. It provides a giant database of conversations and content that can be searched to find patterns in news, subjects talked about, or information about a person or company.

This enhanced ability to communicate is a powerful tool for organizations because a huge part of the success of organizations is communicating with constituents. This could take the form of branding, messaging, sales, relationship building, or simply informing. Once communities began to form, organizations could participate in the community or advertise to the members. This form of advertising has huge benefits because these eCommunities provide the advertiser with concise demographic information on their members.

It's not clear why people are having a hard time accepting that tools like Twitter, text messaging, Facebook, and YouTube are becoming commonplace. It harkens back to the days when people were afraid to use the telephone or when people refused to send e-mail on the computer because it was more comfortable to have something in print and to answer it with notes written on the bottom of the paper. Social tech is simply a variation of tools with specific purposes for enhancing our ability to communicate and connect.

THE POWER OF FACEBOOK

FOR EXAMPLE

Few people realize how deep the demographic data is that Facebook provides to advertisers. Nor do they realize that most of the soon-to-be-over $1 billion in revenues a year that Facebook garners is from selling data to these advertisers. The tradeoff is we get to use Facebook free so we can connect with friends, family, and business contacts on a streaming basis. Organizations are finding many clever ways to leverage Facebook to their hundreds of millions of users. This is a perfect example of the dynamics behind an eCommunity.

Social Relevancy: The (Sometimes Unintended) Outcome of Communication

As mentioned earlier, one of the branches of social technologies is *social relevancy*, which is a different animal than social media or social networking. Social relevancy is all about the online credentials or reputation that gets formed from the content and comments posted about an organization or an individual.

This is a byproduct of all the communication and connection that is now going on. We're creating digital shadows online, and these shadows paint a more detailed picture of us all the time. What others say about us is at least as revealing, or more so, than what we say about ourselves.

The Growing Inventory of Online Content

A typical organization with a Web site has, for the last fifteen years, worked to make sure that when someone types in the firm's name, its Web properties come up at the top of the list. Now we are quickly reaching a point where a search of an organization's name might deliver a stream of mentions on Twitter, YouTube, SlideShare, Scribd, in blogs, and discussion groups, all on the top search page. Their Web site might be at the top of the page, but it's surrounded by snippets of conversations. This now gives a searcher the ability to quickly assess what the *Internet Herd* thinks of a brand or organization.

In addition, any content the organization has published through its "conversations" on Twitter, Facebook, and blogs is quickly visible, as is content posted in social media sites. In other words, it's now possible to develop a quick opinion about an organization by aggregating what you find online that *does not* exist on the organization's Web site. Rather, this

---

DIGITAL SHADOWS

FOR EXAMPLE

In the last year, the top social networking sites have agreed to let Google and others tap into their entire stream of user conversations. For example, Twitter now provides its entire daily stream of tweets to companies that wish to purchase the rights to them. The U.S. Library of Congress has decided to archive every tweet that has ever been done in a database for public access. This means that if your name has ever been mentioned by one of your friends or coworkers on Twitter (or some of the other top sites) anyone interested in you can do a simple Google search and get a glimpse into your life. Add to this any content you've posted online, and that picture of how you think, what you do, and where you are just gets clearer. This is what we mean by casting online digital shadows.

---

information is supplied by people who have come in contact with the organization or are individuals within the organization who have posted thoughts and opinions. The fact that firms can no longer control the message has deep impact on the brand, the reputation, and the ability to sell products for companies.

The Internet Herd (aka The Crowd) Social tech provides many ways to leverage the power of the **KEY TERM** scale of the Internet user base. The 1.8 billion people now online continue to grow quickly. They are collectively referred to as "the crowd," or the Internet Herd. This is important to understand when we talk later in this book about leveraging this crowd through the practice of crowdsourcing.

The same situation exists for people in general. When you search the name of a fellow employee, a sales prospect, or a job candidate, you can access a growing database of information provided by that person, and more importantly, by people around them. By reviewing the content a person has posted, people's reactions to that content, the number of people the person is connected with, and the comments made by others about this person, you can often literally establish their credentials.

Posting Is Forever, and You Need to Be Listening!

Because we're in the early stages of using these new social tools, few people realize that what they post is forever, searchable, and public. This has led to well-publicized stories of people losing jobs, opportunities, and friends over

SMART

MANAGING

MONITORING YOUR ONLINE RELEVANCE

Many tools can help you discover what your online presence is like. These include Web sites like klout.com, socialmention.com, and twittalyzer.com. Smart managers monitor their own online relevancy and work to improve their influence. These tools also help you understand the importance of your online reputation.

what they posted without giving much thought to the repercussions. Recently, a young woman blogged a negative comment about a company that was holding an annual convention at her employer's hotel. The besmirched company ran a listening campaign online and immediately spotted their name in a negative blog. They called the manager of the hotel and complained, and the employee was summarily fired.

We talk more about online reputations later in the book. The takeaway from this early mention of social relevancy is that it is critical to manage your online reputation and that of your employees. Perhaps you're thinking that maybe you'll try to separate yourself from all of this by staying as far away as you can from online sites. It's not a positive thing to be invisible online, and the truth is you won't be able to stop others from talking about you. We need to learn how to find what is said, and manage the positive and negative content as best we can.

All this newfound capability has come to us because we've mixed our desire for connection and communication with the digital plumbing system that is the Internet. History has shown that what we crave as human beings, we often figure out how to supply. We wanted to fly, and we learned how. We wanted to move quickly from place to place, and we coinvented the automobile. We wanted to be entertained in our homes, and we created radio and TV. We wanted to cook meals quickly and developed the microwave. We want to cure all disease, and we're making a dent in that. We have missed the boat on developing a vegetable that tastes like rum raisin ice cream, but who knows, maybe that will be next. We wanted an instant and robust ability to talk to any other human one-to-one, or one-to-many, anywhere in the world—for free. Now we have it.

Along with that, we've created an archive of conversations and content that has turned the word "privacy" upside down. Instead of seeking

TMOI—Too Much Online Information

In the excitement to join the social tech world, some neophytes forget that whatever they post online is permanent, searchable, and public. There are many stories of people discussing their upcoming vacations online only to come back and find their houses ransacked. Or the people who over-share details of their personal life that end up haunting them when they apply for jobs. A new area of TMOI is people posting negative comments about their employer or a customer during online discussions only to learn that these organizations run alerts on any mention of their names.

to hide information from the rest of the world, we'll need to provide lots of information about our thoughts and actions so we can move forward in our careers and connect to people who are looking for us. This may sound like heresy to people who have grown up for years being taught to hide personal information, but the truth is the game is changing, and it's not going back to the way it was. Another truth is that some people go way too far in providing information and lack the discretion to see that certain facts are dangerous to supply to the world.

Why It's Critical to Actively Manage Social Tech Usage at Work

With all these new capabilities being brought to work by users, we're seeing a lot of chaos inside organizations as to how managers and employees use and govern social tech. An unfettered ability to communicate and connect is shaking up how people work, how they talk to each other inside the organization, and how content is provided internally and externally. We lack the rules, mores, and regulations to assure that these powerful tools benefit the organization instead of drain it.

You're standing in the breach. Harnessing the power of social technology is going to happen as millions of managers execute important leadership tasks to help their people learn and integrate these tools. The first job is to put in place cultural rules for how people access and use social tools at work. The second is to document and institutionalize the policies for communicating externally with social tools. Finally, you'll need to provide the vision and training so employees learn to appropriately leverage this

TRICKS OF THE TRADE

EMPLOYEE FACT FINDING
The first thing a smart manager does to get control of social tech is to meet with team members and survey them on what tools they're using. This includes gaining an understanding of the software services they use daily and the devices they use. It's critical to understand what online platforms they're comfortable with and whether they're using company computers or their own mobile devices to access these services. You also want to get a sense of how much time they spend a day using social tools.

growing inventory of tools. If managers don't perform these tasks, organizations will stumble around for years trying to figure out what this field is all about.

Executives are quickly learning that they need to deal with social tech as a trend, and most of them are struggling to find ways to leverage it or "protect" the organization from its use. It's up to you, working in the trenches, to help the executives learn what's going on with the staff, and at the same time, provide good counsel and guidance to their direct reports. To the extent that executives make decisions on a set of tools they may have no experience with, good outcomes will be hard to find. You cannot judge the worth of a social tech tool if you don't use it yourself.

The Role You Must Play

The positive role you can play is being the go-between with staff and executives on the value and potential of social tech. Many executives have an irrational fear that young people will spend all day texting, updating their Facebook profile, twittering with friends, and watching YouTube videos. Managers who understand social technology are in the unique position of being able to judge if the time spent by their people using social tech tools is benefiting the organization or killing productivity.

We can benefit from an analogous example of a technology and examining how we learned to leverage its strengths and minimize its distractions. In this case, let's look at the Web in general. In the mid '90s to the year 2000, we dealt with people excitedly finding thousands of interesting uses for the Web in organizations. We also found fantasy football and porn. Many organizations blocked Internet usage, limited it to a few Web sites, or found safety in allowing only a few people access. We quickly learned that we couldn't throttle this tool by denying all access, because people either found a way to get it or had to use it to access tools other people were providing online. We eventually settled on models such as blocking porn and gambling sites or opening up usage and monitoring it for abuses.

The lesson we should have learned from our first time around with Web 1.0 is that it isn't wise to block all usage of tools that are potentially powerful positives for the organization. We also should have learned that you must monitor usage to assure that people do not abuse access. Like any other tool that has the ability to be wildly productive or dangerously distracting, the use must be managed.

Social technologies will likely change our lives and work patterns more than we can imagine. We're only a few years into the social tech phenomenon. We have many years to go before we have normalized its use (though with the continuous change of technology, that may never be the case). Now is the time to take control of this powerful set of tools and point them and their users in directions beneficial for our organizations!

Manager's Checklist for Chapter 1

☑ Social tech isn't a fad: it's a powerful trend. Don't wait a moment longer to get in front of it.

☑ The desire to have new ways to communicate and less expensive ways to transmit information globally are driving adoption.

☑ There are three areas under the umbrella of social tech: social relevancy, social media, and social networking. You need to understand the differences among these.

☑ The field of social tech is broader than most people realize, and many departments and companies are quickly adopting it as a tool. It's no longer just a sales and marketing concept. Regardless of the area managed, you're faced with finding positive ways to integrate it into your operation.

☑ There is a growing amount of content online about your organization and about you, personally. This requires new ways to monitor what's being said.

☑ Some of that content is being posted by your employees, and they'll sometimes post more information than they should.

☑ It's critical that you as the manager get control of the social tools at the employee level. You're in the best position to gain clarity on how the team is using the tools, and to guide them in using the tools productively.

Chapter

2

Social Technology and the Organization

efore we address best practices for managing social tech, we need to look at how it's being used inside our institutions. Technology has a way of infiltrating businesses and organizations through several avenues. Sometimes tech comes in the front door because the organization purchases new applications or hardware and legislates its use by the team. More often, it's brought in the back door (figuratively), as team members simply bring a new device or application to work and teach others to use it. To understand this backdoor dynamic, we can go back almost 30 years and look at what happened with personal computers, as this was the dawn of technology creeping in through the back door.

Setting a Historical Perspective

Once upon a time the world was ruled by mainframes, and they happened to be big and expensive so none of us could really afford to have one at home. We did what we were told by the IT department, and they gave us two choices—amber or green (the screen color for your terminal). That hegemony was broken when personal computers came into use in the early '80s. Once we had the possibility of choosing our computing device, we also quickly received choices in what software we would run. For 15 years or so, we reveled in the ability to load any piece of software we could get on our 5¼-inch floppy drive, and later on the slick 3.5 inch-diskette.

The Internet upped the ante because it gave us a simple way to download software anytime we wanted. It then became hard for an IT department to control the tools people wanted to use and did use. What we often see is a few people who are "early adopters," who love to discover and test new tools. These people pass on their observations and opinions to their friends, who pass them on yet again. This word-of-mouth system often defeats the organization's desire to limit or control technology proliferation. That's because people will share their ideas and tools in a viral way—whether the institution approves or not. And at times, it's a good thing the rules get bent, because without that happening new capabilities would often be left outside until competitors paved the way!

KEY TERM   **Viral** A descriptor for an idea, piece of media, or technology tool that grows exponentially as people share the information with their friends. Where that once meant a few people you might talk to that day, it now means the thousands of people you are connected to online directly or indirectly through your contacts. Hence this term, like a biological virus, suggests how the awareness of new things can grow exponentially in just a few days.

It's critical for you to understand this grassroots dynamic of technology infiltration because social tech is taking this to a new level. Virtually all social tools come into the organization through early adopters, and in some cases, the tools go viral in a matter of weeks. It takes discretion and wisdom to know when this is a good thing and when it will be counterproductive, and then to manage toward the positive and away from distraction.

Users Choose Their Inventory of Social Tools

Social technology tools by definition are resources that individuals choose based on features they want. Even more than that, they're chosen based on *where* their contacts, friends, and connections hang out. For example, if you have a lot of clients using Twitter, you should probably use Twitter. If they are on LinkedIn, you should be on LinkedIn. For this reason it's difficult for the organization to dictate which social tools a

---

PERSONAL CHOICE AND TECH TOOLS   SMART

We've tried for years to control the technology tools people use. We've done this because we wanted to limit support costs and to keep everyone standard on file types. A smart manager today allows people more flexibility to choose the tools they want to   **MANAGING** use and to institute an understanding that any file they create must be portable to others. In return for this flexibility, people must provide their own support if they have problems with a nonstandard tool. Young people are developing specific skills with specific tools, and it isn't always wise to make them change to a new suite of tools for reasons of standardization.

---

team member should use. This is another reason we see many social applications coming in the companies' back doors. People flock to social sites for reasons that have nothing to do with work, but once there's a large community assembled, employees are tied tightly to it for personal as well as professional reasons.

As much as it might be nerve wracking for organizations to allow people some flexibility in using free, Web-based tools at their own discretion, to do any different is likely futile. There's a growing realization among the enlightened managers that technology is such a powerful enabler, and there are so many alternatives, that we're safe in allowing people to choose the tools they need to do their jobs. Because social tools cross the line between the personal and the professional, they can be seductive in attracting abuse. People are stubborn about moving off an application that they're already using at home when the office wants to use a different system. The free price and easy availability are a blessing and a curse.

USING SOCIAL SITES FOR BOTH PERSONAL AND PROFESSIONAL CONNECTIONS   FOR EXAMPLE

A large regional CPA firm realized that many of the young partners were connecting with clients on their social sites. The knee-jerk reaction was to forbid this practice because of the reputation risks. The problem was that in many cases, the partners were successfully using these social tools to build tighter relationships with the clients. At the same time, the CPA firm was struggling to recruit young CPAs into the organization. They quickly decided to adopt an "if you can't beat 'em, join 'em" attitude and brought in the social tools as a regular piece of the marketing and recruiting process.

SURVEY YOUR DIRECT REPORTS

A good exercise is to formally or informally survey the kinds of social tools your direct reports are using at home and at the office. In many cases, managers are completely unaware of the tools and level of usage away from the office. This can be accomplished in a meeting with everyone on the team and having people tell what they use, and why. Then as a final discussion topic, ask them how they could use social tools to benefit their current jobs.

They erect no barrier to entry for someone to find a tool they like better than what you're using at the office.

Where Social Tech Is Being Used in the Organization

Without attracting much attention, social tech is being picked up and used in many parts of organizations. Most of the early applications came in the back door as people installed tools on their work computers that they were using on their personal machines. There are now many organizations where social tech is being used in a more institutional way, and keep in mind, this is a young set of tools (literally, just a few years old). To gain the proper perspective on how pervasive social tech is already, we've assembled a handful of areas that are leveraging the tools:

- **Marketing.** This may be the first place people think of where social tools provide value. Companies are using Twitter to provide a running conversation with customers and prospects, Facebook to provide information and resources, and YouTube to deliver viral videos. There are many examples in this area because social tools allow organizations to have a nearly free way to communicate with a huge audience—unfiltered by the traditional means of delivery for marketing, like newspapers, magazines, television, or radio. It has never been so easy to target an audience by demographic or to reach them for such a small amount of money per contact.
- **Sales.** To close a sale, you must first build a level of trust between the purchaser of your product and the company. This is true for any level of simplicity or complexity. To find someone to sell to, you first have to identify him or her as a legitimate prospect. Social tools can fill both of these roles. Sophisticated searching and online demographics can

help you identify likely customers. Social communication tools and eWord of mouth can help you build trust. Providing links with coupons or discounts embedded in social tech conversations can drive customers to a Web site to facilitate the sale.

---

eWord of Mouth: Traditional word of mouth has always been the most powerful source of persuasion in getting a product or service sold. People trust their friends more than advertising. Most studies show that around 13 percent of consumers **KEY TERM** believe advertising and 80 percent believe word-of-mouth recommendations. Social tech now gives us the ability to generate and nurture electronic word of mouth. This can be done by giving people tools like videos, links, and electronic documents that they pass to their friends to promote things they believe in. You'll see us shorten the moniker for this concept to eWord of mouth from now on.

- **Virtual teams.** As more organizations allow people to work remotely and assemble teams made up of people in different offices, the concept of virtual teams is growing. One of the driving factors in this concept has been the technological ability for remote workers to communicate seamlessly. Social tools have added to our ability to allow workers to build relationships and communicate over distances. (For more on this see *Managing Virtual Teams* by Kimball and Mareen Fisher, another title in the Briefcase Books series.)

  Virtual Teams Whenever an organization assembles teams where one or some members don't physically **KEY TERM** work where the rest of the team works, this creates a virtual team. This can range from a couple of members working from home or remotely, to an entire team where each member is in a different location.

- **Internal communications.** For teams of any size to function productively, they must be able to communicate well. Breakdowns in communication are probably the number one source of friction on any team. The number one benefit of social tools is the improved ability for people to communicate. This includes helping the organization improve the flows of general information to help everyone make better decisions.

- **Personal networking.** We have long used the term "having a good Rolodex" as a metaphor for someone who has lots of contacts and relationships that can be leveraged when needed. Now that the Rolodex is a thing of the past, we have "friends, followers, and contacts" as replacements. Social tools enable a team member to build an electronic "Rolodex" with thousands of people whom they can reach out to, and this "Rolodex" never gets out of date or lost.
- **Information gathering.** Social tools have provided an outstanding way to gather real-time information on subjects that are critical to the organization. This could be industry facts and happenings, competitive information, or customer satisfaction comments being made online. We've simply never had such a powerful means of gathering information with a few tools and searches. The prime example of this is the information that human resources departments now gather on prospective employees before they ever show up for an interview.
- **Crowdsourcing.** Many organizations are starting to use the Internet Herd to do work that had traditionally been done in-house or through a vendor. This is providing a lower-cost solution and a faster way to get work done. This concept is being used across areas in many firms already. We discuss crowdsourcing in more detail later in the book, so if you're unfamiliar with how this is being done, read on.

Frictionless and Free Communication Is the Key

Let's wrap this up by acknowledging that organizations have a better chance of being successful when they communicate well internally and externally. Add to that the skill of collaboration and an ability to leverage online resources, and you have a good base to work from. These areas are the very things that social tools improve when implemented and used correctly. They are not one-to-one applications that people use for personal communications. They have infiltrated our organizations, and we won't be able to go back to the way it was before.

Still . . . we have a high percentage of companies that block people from using these tools at work. Is this wise? Should we close off people's ability to use their personal tools at work, especially when the line between personal and professional is so blurred? Unfortunately, many are throwing the baby out with the bathwater as they try to block all social tech usage at work.

Leveraging or Blocking Social Tech Tools?

> **KEY TERM**
>
> **Blocking** When we refer to an organization blocking social technology use, we mean that the IT department configures the routers and switches so that specific Web sites cannot be accessed from the company network.

Whether organizations should block social tools or not is a hotly debated topic among technology and human resource professionals these days. Recent research shows that more than half of all organizations block sites typically thought of as social networking or social media properties. Some are even blocking sites like LinkedIn, which shows a complete lack of understanding of how these tools are being used.

This demonstrates how perplexed many organizations are with the concept of social tools. We have everything from early adopters who are proving that it can have a dramatic impact on the bottom line, to companies that do everything they can to stop anyone from using it. What a mess!

> **FOR EXAMPLE**
>
> **SALES LEADS AND LINKEDIN**
>
> In a recent discussion with a salesperson at a large software company, the subject of LinkedIn came up. He related an event that had just happened to him. A contact on LinkedIn who was a former colleague inquired about the services this salesperson sells today. The company that his ex-coworker had gone to work for would never have come up on the radar as a sales prospect, but because of the connection that existed with LinkedIn, the salesperson was in a good position to close another sale.

Should We or Should We Not Mix Personal and Professional Use?

The question of who's right and who's wrong in this debate is complicated. The people who vote for wide open use of social tools believe they enhance productivity by letting people tap their friends and the collective social sphere for help and knowledge when needed. They also point out that to learn how to use social tools well for the benefit of the organization, people need to know how to use them personally. Then they'll be able figure out how they apply to reaching organizational goals.

USING A PERSONAL NETWORK

FOR EXAMPLE

Jill is a 25-year-old employee of a large manufacturing company. Her job is to develop the Web-based tie-ins to the traditional marketing methods used by her company. This includes coordinating activities among the company's catalogs, trade shows, and marketing materials. One day while reviewing the photographs being used on a specific ad, she noticed a picture that she thought might offend many women. Her manager disagreed and planned to move forward until Jill sent a copy of the ad to her network and asked for opinions. In a matter of minutes she was able to prove that the photo would be an issue. It was her command of social networking that allowed her to quickly poll people whom she could trust to give valuable advice.

The people who believe that all social networking/media use should be blocked tend to cite the following arguments: first, it entices people to waste lots of time on personal communications when they should be focused on work. Second, it's a security nightmare because it gives the IT department a new open door for bad guys to use in computer attacks. Third, it's easy for people to leak important company information to the public. And finally, it facilitates people being able to find a new job whenever they get unhappy with anything.

A Helpful Guide for Making Usage Decisions

To decide on the best practices for an organization, many factors have to be taken into account. At the same time, managers need to clearly understand and support the institutional guidelines and reasoning behind decisions governing the use of social tools. For most organizations the answer lies somewhere between blocking and completely open use. Let's look at a few factors that should influence what the best path is for your organization.

- **The job descriptions that dominate the location.** If you have a location or company that's predominantly manufacturing, warehouse, or blue-collar workers, it might make more sense to limit usage. To the extent that the workforce is more white-collar, you would find that access to social tools can be a plus in helping employees be more productive.
- **Your workforce demographic.** The younger your workforce is, the more likely you'll create a negative culture by blocking the tools these

PROMISCUOUS CLICKING

FOR EXAMPLE

It took computer security people years to get employees to quit opening suspicious files they receive in e-mails. In some cases, viruses still get into systems from people who click on links that should be left alone. Travis was not thinking about this when he received a tweet on Twitter with the heading "Great picture of you—bitly.com/23514." Travis loves to see his own pictures, so he clicks on the link and goes to a Web page with a file that needs to be opened in order to see his picture. He opens the file and strangely, the picture isn't of him. In fact it's a female. Odd, but he does not think anything more about it as he goes on with his work. Little does he know that he just turned loose a piece of malware into the company network.

employees see as essential. The older the workforce, the less they'll resist access controls. The only problem with this dynamic is that people tend to apply it in reverse. We want to block young people from using the tools because we know they're heavy users, and we want to allow access by older people who we feel have more discretion and would use the tools appropriately. This thinking is actually backwards.

- **The need for information restriction.** The more regulated your company is or the more sensitive organizational information is, the more you might be led to restrict usage. I've talked to military and government employees who point out to me how dangerous it is in just telling people what they do for a living. The less regulated or secretive you are, the less you have to worry about information being exposed.

- **Your sales and marketing model.** For companies that deal with consumer products and have a selling model that includes a heavy amount of branding and eWord of mouth, it makes sense to allow usage. You should encourage access so your employees use social tools to promote good information online and monitor what's being said about your company. If your company has a sales force that sells products or services directly to consumers, it makes sense to allow salespeople open access to any social tools that will help them find prospects and close sales.

- **Past history of use or abuse.** If your experience with the Web ten years ago was bad—in other words, people were distracted and spent a lot of time on inappropriate sites, then you might consider restricting usage. If your team was generally responsible, then you can assume they'll also be responsible using social tools.

- **Use by the customer base.** This may be one of the most important factors in making the decision. If your customer base is a heavy user of social tools, there is little question that you need to have more open access. If the people you sell to are not generally using social sites, you have less of a reason to give employees access.

If you think that blocking social tech use will keep you safe from any of the negative aspects listed earlier, think again. There are a number of factors working against organizations that go in this direction. The first, and most dangerous, is that many people carry mobile devices that have full access to the Internet, and there are specific applications that let users connect to their social sites completely out of reach of the organization.

CAUTION

FORCING PEOPLE TO GO MOBILE

The last thing you want to do is block people from using social tools on the company computers only to have them go onto their mobile devices. You'll find they'll spend more time on their mobile devices because they know you're not monitoring this activity. If you monitor use instead of blocking it, they'll tend to use their office computer and then you'll at least be aware of the appropriateness of the time spent online.

Two Important Options

This leaves us with two practical solutions for you to consider. The first solution is to routinely block use of social media/networking sites unless employees can show they have a legitimate use for the tools. Leave this decision to the management level of the organization. They can approve direct reports using their discretion based on their relationship and observations of the user. This provides protections from abuse while giving freedom to people who have legitimate uses for the tools.

The second possible solution is to open access to everyone, but run monitoring software that tracks site usage. Assign someone in the HR department to review the logs every month so you can see how much time employees spend on the social sites. If you see an excessive amount of time on social sites, you can deal with it on a one-to-one basis. This has the advantage of keeping people off their mobile devices yet allowing someone the flexibility to use the tool for beneficial purposes.

Monitoring Software
Monitoring applications log what each user is doing on the Web. This includes **KEY TERM** what sites they go to and how long they stay on each site. The system generates reports that detail this information so it's possible to see who is abusing usage.

Generations, the Organization, and Social Tech

We can probably agree that due to the influences each generation has experienced they have different world views and varying levels of willingness to learn new things. They also have contrasting levels of comfort and proficiency with the software and devices that are prevalent in organizations today. Recent social tool demographics show that the average age of users is nearing 38, and that surprises many people. The fact is that older people will adopt technology tools once they see a clear value. Younger people tend to adopt new tools faster because they are more willing to experiment and have less history of using other tools.

Any generalization of the habits of the four generations is going to be wrong at some level, but for the purposes of a basic understanding, here's how each generation views new technologies.

Gen Y, or the Millennials

This generation has never known a time without the Web. They are getting access to mobile devices as teens (or younger) and are completely comfortable with the lack of privacy in the social tech realm. They adopt new hardware and software easily, and in fact, get bored using the same tools for months in a row. They can't wait to change to something new. They are forever looking for increases in speed, functionality, battery time, and the cool factor.

They tend to flock to new software when their friends invite them, and take it as a badge of pride when they know more than their friends about how applications work. From a work standpoint, they love finding new ways to be more productive, and this may be driven by their generally suspect work ethic. If a piece of technology can help them get eight hours of work done in five, then they figure they have that much more of their day to relax. They believe every problem has a solution online, if a person can use search capabilities well enough. It's a natural habit for them to reach out to their electronic network when they have questions, need an opinion, or need a job.

They are very attached to their devices. To be without a smart phone or their laptop is akin to being naked in the world. These devices are quickly becoming their outboard brain. They feel less without access to Internet connectivity and instant access to communication with their network.

Generation X

This generation had personal computers when they were young so they have grown up with a technology-enabled world, and during much of their careers have had access to the Web as a tool. They have little fear of technology but don't crave it or seem to be as addicted to new tech as the younger Gen Ys.

Gen Xers quickly adopt any technology that looks like it might help their career or is being adopted by a lot of the Gen Ys. Because Gen Xers are old enough to have families, careers, homes, and responsibilities, they get frustrated when their technology takes too much time to learn. They lack the time to experiment, so they want applications to be easy to understand in a short time.

Gen Xers are struggling mightily with the issues of combining personal and professional contacts in the social space. Since many of their friends might also do business with them, and most are connecting through social networking sites, this generation struggles more than any other with this dilemma. Gen Xers love to stay current, and want to keep up with their kids. They are concerned about what their kids are doing with technology, and how it impacts them. Because they're the first generation to grow up with lots of personal tech, they're also the first to deal with kids having it even earlier than they did. Combine this with their driving need to have a friendly relationship with their kids, and you have a real social struggle.

Baby Boomers

This group didn't grow up with technology. They were well into their careers in many cases before the PC came out. For some, the Internet still seems like a magical tool. That's because they remember working for years without having the instant ability to do a search and get an answer to virtually any question. Some people in this generation have a little fear of technology since it hasn't been a big part of their lives; therefore, they have to be shown that there's a clear return on a time or money investment on a new tool or concept. This is also a generation that is deep into their careers, often at some level of management, busy, and without time to do lots of experimentation.

Traditionals (the Great Generation)

This generation is predominantly over 65 years old, and the use of social tools varies widely based on whether they are in their careers or retired. For those still in the marketplace, social tools are a kind of mystery. They don't personally use them at a high rate or have many friends who use them. If they're retired, they actually have a better chance of using these tools because they have the time to experiment and are willing to see them as ways to keep in touch with kids, grandkids, and others. This generation above all others must have a clear reason or inspiration for dedicating time to social tools. This often comes from a desire to connect with people who ask them to use social tools because they prefer this method of keeping in touch.

As a manager, it's critical to play the role of translator among all the generations. For the younger generation, you must help them understand that not everyone does 100 texts a day or uses Facebook and Twitter constantly. And the funny thing is, older generations can still be good at their jobs even without

> **REVERSE MENTORING** **SMART**
>
> A wonderful technique for bringing the generations together is the concept of **MANAGING** reverse mentoring. This is a process whereby you match an older team member with a young, tech-savvy person for the purpose of knowledge transfer from young to old. Not only is this effective for spreading social tech knowledge, it also helps build relationships that will pay off in many other areas.

YouTube. Gen X and Y discount the older generations' value because they think they are out of touch for not using social tools that clearly can be productive.

For older people, you often have to explain why a new technology has value. They make their decisions to invest time learning a new technology carefully and there has to be clear value. What they struggle with is making value judgments about how Gen Y operates. The older generations assume that any time spent on smart phones, or Facebook is a waste of time. Without a good leader to bridge the gap between generations, there can be a gulf in understanding, and that isn't good for team dynamics.

The Dangers of Serving Only One Generation

This generational difference in views can create an issue with blocking social tools across the whole network. Gen X and Gen Y use these tools like the older generations use a calculator. We have a generation that sees little differentiation between in-person friends, online friends, coworkers, and contacts. These are all relationships or connections to be used for different reasons at various times. They are also all potential resources that can help young people with their jobs. The difficult dynamic we face today is that an older generation is in charge of organizations and generally is slower to adopt social tools. This has set up a divide of understanding that causes conflict in the organization's culture.

It's important that you keep your fingers on the pulse of what tools your young hires are using when they come to work and make good judgments before requiring them to operate differently. IT departments have valid reasons for setting standards for software use. At the same time, we are moving into a world where formats are portable, data adheres to universal standards, and the software application provider is getting less important. An interesting example of this is the number of college students coming into the workforce who use Google Docs as their main word processor or spreadsheet application. They come into organizations that have standardized on Microsoft Office, and the conflict begins.

The Potential of Social Tech

Technology has proven to be a catalyst for either positive or negative impacts on organizational culture, depending on how its proliferation is

HR MAKES THE CALL ON FACEBOOK

A large U.S.-based defense contractor recently opened up access to Facebook across the organization after having it blocked for a long time. When asked why they opened it up, the HR department commented that when they brought a good young engineer on board and then told him or her that they blocked all social tools, the company appeared to be in the Stone Age. This was reason enough for some of them to move on to "cooler" companies. Once it was clear what the contractor was losing by blocking Facebook, they decided the risk of having it available was less than the sure thing of losing good young people.

handled. We saw the same dynamic with personal computers and then the Internet. Companies that moved toward heavy use of e-commerce often struggled with an old guard that felt out of place as they watched the percentage of online sales climb. They had spent much of a career learning to drive revenue in one basic model—now there was a new model in town.

Social tech has the same potential as the major technical break-throughs that have gone before. If we're to learn anything from the past, it's that we need to mainstream the use of these tools across the generations so we don't create a have-and-have-not situation. The sooner the entire organization can learn what the social tech movement is all about, what the valuable concepts and ideas are, and how to leverage these into progress, the better. This takes strong and visionary leadership, and that is what we discuss in the next chapter.

Manager's Checklist for Chapter 2

☑ Social tech is going to impact how many people get work done. It will have the same level of reach that word processing and spreadsheets have as a business tool, and will also be as common. Social tech integration into the organization needs to be managed well in the early stages.

☑ Social tools will be the difference between success and failure for some organizations. That may sound strong, yet it's realistic. Social tools are already having a big impact on a company's revenue streams and will only grow as a sales and marketing tool. For industries undergoing big changes in their business models, learning to use social tech better than their competitors may be a lifesaver.

☑ Social tech isn't going away; it isn't a fad and it will only grow. This isn't an inventory of tools you can ignore for a few years. Regardless of what industry you're in, there are concepts and ideas that could help your organization.

☑ Most organizations are in chaos with social tech at the moment. Because the usage and adoption has grown so much so quickly, businesses are struggling to figure out how to fit it into their strategies. It's up to the managers/leaders to actively step in and sort out what's appropriate use and what can provide awesome results.

☑ Trying to block or deny use of social tools across the board is unwise. You must have usage policies that protect the organization from abuse, yet allow access to the people who really can leverage these tools. You must also monitor usage so you spot abuse among those who have access.

☑ The four generations in the workforce at the moment generally view and use social tools differently; you must account for that and help each with their unique issues. You must find ways to bring together young power users and older, experienced team members who could leverage these tools.

Setting the Tone: Social Tech from a Leadership Perspective

You'll see a recurring theme in regard to the importance of providing outstanding leadership when it comes to integrating social technologies into the organization. These tools have such huge promise, and at the same time, can be devastatingly distracting or dangerous when misused. There will be an adoption curve over the next ten years and until we get through that and standardize their use, social tools will require a lot of oversight and guidance. Let's take a look at some of the philosophies that will help you lead your people to positive use of these tools.

It's a truism that leading by example is the most powerful way to move people. People naturally follow what a leader *does* more than what a leader *says*. Technology tools are a challenge to this dynamic because leaders are often older than those who follow them, and their comfort level for new tech tools is lower. Or maybe it's more true to say that the younger that people are, the more fearless and motivated they are to learn new technologies.

This dynamic is why we highlighted the concept of reverse mentoring in the last chapter. Productive use of new technologies is an area where young people can mentor older employees. Even so, to be an effective leader, you must be willing to invest time and energy into using social tech tools so that others will see you as a role model.

SYMBOLIC ATTEMPTS

Be careful about making symbolic attempts to use social tools. Simply signing up for a number of new sites, then putting little energy into using them is worse than not signing up at all. A common mistake managers make is to sign up for something like Facebook, fill out the profile, connect to a couple of friends, and then fail to return to the site. This gives employees a mixed message as to whether they should be using a tool like this.

If you want to be a great example for others, here's a suggestion. Pick out one social tech tool at a time, learn how to use it *completely*. Then connect with others so they can see how it's done. In many cases, they might be ahead of you, and your proper use of the tool will be validation for them as to what you expect. It's better to be really productive with five social tech tools, than to be a signer upper on ten different sites. Here are more helpful hints on becoming a great example:

Connect with everyone. When you've chosen to get proficient with something like LinkedIn, Facebook, Foursquare, SlideShare, or Twitter, connect with everyone you can in your contact network. If the system is a social networking site, see how many contacts accept an invitation. If the site is a social media site and you're uploading content, send the link out to everyone you know so they can see what you're doing and send a reply. In many cases, there's no reason to distinguish between personal and professional contacts because your personal contacts are often interested in what you're doing in your career. The same is *not* true in the other direction. When you upload personal pictures of your latest grandchild to Flickr, it's best to select a few family and friends to receive the link.

Know system features. Take time to study the administration features of the system, what options you have for privacy, security, automatic notifications, and user interface layout. Many of these systems have a complete ability to control your usage and others' access to your information, but you won't know this unless you invest some time learning the features.

Fill out the profile. Fill out your profile completely and keep the information business-appropriate. Many systems allow your profile information to be searchable so if someone tries to find you on the Web, they'll often get your Facebook, LinkedIn, or Twitter profile in the first results page. An

> **User Interface** Many systems give you the option to "decorate" your profile or page. From a business standpoint, how you use this capability says a lot about you. If you leave the default background and look, you mark yourself as a new and **KEY TERM** unsophisticated user. Twitter is a good example because you can add a custom background with your contact information so that your user interface becomes like a business card for contacts to find you online. (For an example of a Twitter custom background, go to www.twitter.com/sklososky.)

empty profile looks bad, as does one that mentions your favorite pastime is clubbing baby seals.

Pick your picture. Put some thought into your profile picture. This may seem like a small thing, but it's an area where many leaders look silly. They post pictures that are shot from too far away so the person is unidentifiable. Or they use a picture that's 20 years old. Some people think you should use a symbol instead of a picture, for security reasons. Unless you are Prince and really trying to brand yourself as a symbol, forget that. If you are a woman, please don't use a glamour shot that makes it look as if you're on a Vegas trip. Stick with a close-up, businesslike photo where you are smiling and wearing something you would wear at work.

Using Social Tools with Your Employees

Above all, use the tools you choose to communicate with your people so they see you using them. Nothing provides a better example than using social tech tools to augment your relationships with the people who work for you. Your next question may be "But should I really connect on Facebook and LinkedIn with people who report to me?" The answer to that is, it depends on how you use social networking sites like these. If you connect with personal contacts on Facebook and leave your business contacts on LinkedIn, you may want to connect with employees only on LinkedIn. If you use a Twitter feed or blog to post content that's business related, make sure the people who report to you are signed up so they can see what you're thinking and producing publicly.

I understand that there are security concerns in certain types of organizations, and you may not be able to use the open Internet tools to communicate internal conversations. There are private and secure versions of most capabilities you can get in Twitter, Facebook, and the other publicly available tools. Don't ignore the potential of using social tools because of the word "social." Even highly secure organizations need to provide good communication among employees.

THE SECURITY EXCUSE

CAUTION We've worked with a number of people over the last couple of years who use the fact that they work for law enforcement, the government, the military, or some other security-cleared organization as a reason to not use social tools. The danger with this is that they're making a decision based on seeing social tools as only social networking. Although there are admittedly many services and concepts that don't apply, there are others that do. Keep an open mind about using internally secure applications to perform some of the basic functions and you'll reap the same rewards as the civilian world.

The word "social" causes a perception problem for many managers. Because this word connotes something done personally or something done with people outside the organization, some managers lose site of how beneficial these tools can be to internal communications. There are many social tools built specifically to help closed groups communicate.

There are also communication platforms that can be used internally and externally, such as Skype. Although Skype has grown tremendously, and this year may equal the telephone system in the volume of calls made internationally, there are many firms that waste thousands of dollars that could be saved if they used Skype as a communication system.

There's a saying in the writing business that you have to "show, don't tell." It's the same with social tools. A productive, confident manager shows

YAMMER AND PRIVATE CHAT PLATFORMS

A type of tool that is growing in popularity is the private microblogging platform like Yammer.com. Think of this like Twitter, but for a closed group of people who must be invited by the **TOOLS** administrator to participate. These applications allow dispersed people to have a place where they can talk to each other in a public way. Since a certain percentage of comments or questions are likely to be interesting to a large group, this type of service facilitates these conversations.

people proper use by demonstrating it, paying attention to the details, and fully exploiting the features in whatever platform is used. To ignore social tech as a powerful tool is to be ignorant. To promote its use and then not use it personally is a step better, but this still makes you a hypocrite.

COMMUNICATING REMOTELY WITH SKYPE

FOR EXAMPLE

A vice-president of international relations for a large association spent his career using a phone as his primary tool for talking to offices overseas. Because he did this, his people from all over the world followed his example. Many of them, when asked, said they didn't understand why he wasn't using Skype to communicate because they were all proficient with this *free* tool. Our VP was also racking up phone bills in excess of $3,000 a month, which could have been put to better use.

The Dangers of Managing Employees Through Social Tools

Let's draw an important distinction here. Using social tools with your people does not mean *managing* them through these tools. There is a fine line between using social tools to communicate with your direct reports, and using these tools to have conversations that need to take place in person. People should know this from the same dynamic that has arisen when people try to manage inappropriately through e-mail. These text-based forms of communication can't provide facial expressions and tone of voice or the ability to truly have an interactive conversation. Some people might think this is an old-school concept, but let's discuss why a good manager would choose to have certain discussions in person rather than through a Web-based application.

There is a component of management that is coordinating activities. This is a perfect place to use technology. When it comes to other components, like counseling employees about sub-par performance, the face-to-face approach works better. This is because humans tend to be emotionally attached to other people's perceptions of them. This is especially true when that other person is your manager and holds the power of advancement or even continued employment. There are times when you as manager need to explain to someone why he or she has missed the mark. It's critical that your message not only guides the person to new behavior, but also leaves this employee in an emotional place where he or she wants to make progress. Sometimes this can only come through clarification of examples and details around the issue.

Text-based online communication often lacks the context or detail to fully leave the receiving person in a good place. It's really difficult to inspire people through Web applications. It's done better face to face. Now that we have the ability to send messages in many formats and platforms, i.e., text messaging, Twitter, Yammer, Facebook, or LinkedIn, we must walk the line between using these systems to transfer information and ask questions, but not managing through them.

Just be careful any time you're going to make a comment that concerns someone's performance if the input is some form of counseling. If you're going to praise someone, doing it in "writing" through a social tool is normally fine, especially if you're allowing other people to see the praise. Whenever possible, most people will be more pumped up with a literal pat on the back and looking into your eyes when you tell them "good job." If you're going to point out to them something they're doing wrong, they'll better understand the context and importance of what you say if they can talk to you in person. This also gives them the chance to ask questions, verify what correction is expected, and get on down the road without the counseling becoming a huge emotional issue.

> **TRICKS OF THE TRADE**
>
> **VIRTUAL MANAGEMENT**
>
> There is one caveat to using social tools as a delivery vehicle when your people need to be counseled, and that is when you have no choice because of a virtual team layout. If you have no option to meet with a person face to face, you might think a phone call is the next best thing. Actually, using video call capabilities might be a better choice. This allows the other person to at least be able to add the context of your facial expressions, body language, and eye contact to the conversation.

The Importance of Setting Individual Goals for Your People

One of the important things you should do as a leader is to set goals and expectations regarding social tech. Because this is such a new tool and it's often fuzzy as to how it can be leveraged, you can do your people a huge favor by stating clear and concise goals for them. Don't only set general organizational goals for all your people (such as everyone using a specific tool), but also set individual goals for each of them in their specific positions.

Let's look at an example. If you're in charge of a group of salespeople, it would be a great idea to set a goal for them on how many connections they should have through their social sites. This is a new-generation measurement of their networking abilities. For instance, set a goal of 1,000 connections as the bar that you expect every salesperson to be at by year end. This is smart because it requires them to think about how they'll find people to connect with and motivates them to learn how to expand their network in valuable ways.

As a second step, you can give each of them specific goals for what you expect them to accomplish by using this network. If someone is a big game sales hunter and he or she specializes in major accounts, you might give this person a goal of finding connections in the Fortune 500 list. If another salesperson specializes in selling to government accounts, he or she would have a different goal, such as identifying and connecting with as many people as possible in one department.

The Positive and Negative with Goals

In a new field like social tech, it can sometimes be difficult to figure what types of goals are valuable. Goals can be positive or negative tools. On the positive side, they can guide us toward the results we wish to achieve. They provide the touchstone that we can reach for every day so that we

---

GOAL QUALITY OR QUANTITY

Be careful when you set goals to consider quality over quantity. You don't want to drive a dynamic where people are simply meeting your volume goals but the actual value is nil because of quality. For example, you could set a goal of creating a certain volume of content on a blog or Twitter feed, and the salesperson could easily meet it by producing sloppy and boring content. You have now taken a big step backward. Alternatively, if you ask someone to meet an objective such as a volume of connections and the person connects with people who are unhelpful, again, you haven't accomplished much.

know we're making progress. Over time, setting goals has proven to be a beneficial and measurable way to move forward. On the other hand, setting the wrong goals or setting goals without thinking of the consequences of the journey that may be required can be negative instead of positive. For example, a person could set a goal of running a marathon this year, but if the person isn't physically in shape to take that on in the timeframe committed, either he or she will fail or be injured trying to succeed. That goal was ill conceived from the start.

This dynamic applies to social tech because setting aggressive goals might sound great, but to achieve them, people will become distracted from their other tasks. If goals are set intelligently and with consideration, they'll dramatically speed up the learning process of team members. Consider choosing from a few of the goals below for each of your people.

- **Quantity of connections.** A connection is defined as a contact on services like LinkedIn, online friends, or followers of your content (blogs or Twitter, for example). A volume of connections can be leveraged for many interesting uses with social tools, e.g., gathering information, answering questions, and prospecting for customers.

- **Quantity and quality of content provided.** For certain types of jobs it's critical to establish oneself as an industry expert. Providing online ideas and thoughts about a person's specific expertise increasingly does this. Volume of information isn't the only metric that matters, so be careful to have some type of quality measurement, as well.

- **Frequency of content production.** To really create a valuable flow of information or engage readers in an ongoing conversation, it's critical to provide a consistent and frequent stream of information. Goals can easily be set to inspire regular postings.

- **Velocity of connections (per month).** The only issue with the first goal we discussed is that it doesn't take into account the regular growth of the connections a person is getting. At times it's more appropriate to set monthly goals that define the velocity by which you want people to be adding connections. For example, 100 a month, or 10 percent more every month.

- **Number of positive mentions on the Web.** This metric can be useful in measuring how someone is doing with building his or her online reputation. Note the word "positive" because it's not only a matter of being talked about. Negative press might be OK for some Hollywood stars, but for businesspeople it's all about positive comments online.

- **Sentiment ratio.** A companion goal of the previous metric is the ratio of positive to negative comments. There's a third category of sentiment, and that's neutral. When creating a goal around this metric, you must specify the ratio you want among all three.

- **Number of people who have forwarded content.** One great measurement of the quality of content is the number of people who forward links to this content or the content itself to others. This is one of the most positive ways that people vote on the quality of content.

- **Number of click-throughs on links provided.** At times, the content that a person provides can include links to e-commerce systems or promotional systems. Because creating sales prospects is critical to a sales organization, measuring a person's ability to get their contacts to click on links that identify them as prospects or create sales is valuable.

- **Expertise within social applications.** One of the beneficial goals for new users is to give them a list of features you want them to learn about in a specific application. Pick the seven most important things they need to know how to do with LinkedIn, YouTube, Scribd, and SlideShare, for example. Set a deadline to get this done, and they'll be motivated to do more than just sign up and connect with contacts.

As a manager, goal setting is one of your most powerful tools for establishing expectations. It then provides a basis for measuring progress and holding people accountable to hit the target. This is especially important with new team members or with current employees who are set in their ways and difficult to convince to learn new skills. Remember, what gets measured gets

> **MEASUREMENT TOOLS**
>
> For many of these goals you need measurement tools to help you know if a person is making progress. Spend some time and familiarize yourself with the following tools:
>
>
>
> **TOOLS**
>
> - Socialmention.com—Free
> - Klout.com—Free
> - SM2 by Alterian.com—Fee-based
> - Viral Heat—Fee-based
> - Radian6—Fee-based

done. If you never set expectations for people in their use of social tools, they'll often find other priorities and put off learning to use these tools fully.

Let's kick around some additional thoughts in this area.

Onboarding and Helping Employees

As being proficient with social tools becomes more important to employees' ability to communicate with each other, customers, and partners, the need to get new team members up to speed quickly increases. Using the phone system as a metaphor, one of the first things we did when we onboarded an employee was to teach them to use it. We understood that this was the tool for connecting with people internally and externally. Strangely, when we onboard people these days we rarely give them much information about e-mail etiquette, and certainly little about social tech practices. This is backward when these are now by volume more immersive forms of communication in the workplace.

We talk in the next section about creating guidelines and policies for using social tools that can help managers get across to new employees the organizational standards and more. There are also a few other interesting things a manager can do to help people get adjusted quickly.

SMART MANAGING

QUICK INTEGRATION OF NEW EMPLOYEES

There are a number of benefits to helping people more quickly integrate with the culture and mechanics of an organization. Social tools can facilitate people getting to know their workmates more quickly because it provides multiple ways to communicate and access to profile information on those around you. The faster a manager can get someone integrated into the network of social tools, the faster they become familiar with the other team members and team dynamics. This allows them to focus more energy on the work at hand and less on finding their place in the tribe (so to speak).

Determining Proficiency

One of the early things a manager can do when onboarding people is to do a quick check of their proficiency level with social tools and of which platforms they prefer. This includes finding out how large their online network is and their history of creating and posting new content. All this information is useful in guiding them in valuable ways to use these tools at work.

If you discover that social tech skills are lacking, a training strategy can be put in place. There are formal teaching options if the organization offers classes, lunch-and-learn programs, or informal training that can be self-paced by finding how-to manuals online. Here are a few examples of the kinds of how-to blogs you can find by searching:

- **http://mashable.com/2009/09/22/facebook-pages-guide**
- **http://mashable.com/2009/08/14/facebook-networking**
- **http://mashable.com/2009/04/02/facebook-personal-brand**
- **http://mashable.com/2009/01/13/social-media-resume**

One of the best ways to help people get up to speed is to pair them with current team members who are proficient already, because then you get the added benefit of building internal relationships.

Regardless of where new people's skill levels might be, a series of goals can be established to help them either leverage what they already can do with their network or to learn to build one from the ground up. A productive early goal is to have new people use their social tech skills to connect with others on the team. This provides inspiration to the team members who might be lagging and a quick way for those on the same wavelength to get to know each other.

> ### ONBOARDING AND VIRTUAL TEAMS
> **TRICKS OF THE TRADE**
>
> Setting a goal of connecting with your team members through social tech sites is especially helpful when the team has members who are working virtually. This is an excellent way to help them get to know each other when they can't see each other in the breakroom. Absent using social tools to open lines of communication, your only options are phone calls or in-person meetings, and these may not happen frequently enough to build relationships quickly.

Adding Social Tech Measurements to Employee Reviews

Many organizations have a standardized method for doing employee reviews. Adding a measurement benchmark for proficiency with social tools or online content creation is a timely thing to do these days. At both ends of the knowledge spectrum, you will find this helpful. If employees are uncomfortable with these new tools, adding it to their review holds them accountable to get up to speed. If the employee is a wizard with social tech, then adding in metrics that measure the *valuable* usage of his or her social network to the company is a good measurement of progress.

For some of you this might sound excessive, but keep an open mind. There are some positions in the organization where social tech won't be a good fit as an area to be measured. In others, it will be a critical measurement. Again, let's use salespeople as an example. Today and certainly going forward, it's important that salespeople learn the skill of social networking as a means of finding new prospects and building tighter relationships with current customers. In addition, a salesperson must be concerned with his or her online reputation. This is because many buyers now lean toward wanting to buy products and services from a recognized expert, not a peddler. The salesperson's online reputation will be his or her credentials for many buyers—like it or not. For this reason, you can do salespeople a favor by providing an incentive in their evaluations for them to get up to speed with new social tools and manage their online reputations.

Another good example can be found with executive-level people. If you're leading high-level managers as direct reports, social tech measurements should be part of any evaluation. They also need to have a good online reputation to provide solid credentials when business partners check on them online. Other positions where it makes sense to add social tool skills to the employee evaluation include marketing, advertising, project management, corporate communications, information technology, customer service, and product management. All these areas have the potential to leverage social tools to perform their job well.

Setting Internal Policies and Guidelines

One of the most important tools in the manager's leadership toolkit in the area of social tech is the organization's written governance policies and best practices. If your firm does not have a written policy document, your first step should be to help them get one in place.

No organization should function without some kind of written policy that states the rules, boundaries, mores, and best practices for using social tools. According to a recent Manpower survey, only 29 percent of organizations have a written social tech policy at the moment. The absence of a written guideline can cause chaos among the team because each individual will set his or her own standards and, in some cases, that can negatively impact the team as a whole.

The Elements of a Solid Social Tech Policy Document

If you have no experience in creating a social tech governance document, let's take a look at some of the areas it should cover:

- **Proper use at work.** This helps employees understand how much time is appropriate to spend using social tools or if they are allowed to at all. This can also be used to make general statements as to how specific tools may be used in beneficial ways.
- **Proper configuration of online profiles.** This helps employees assemble profiles with appropriate pictures and information so that customers are not offended.
- **Rules for engaging in conversations with clients.** This makes it clear to team members the preferred style, methods, tone, and substance of communications with the people who keep you in business.
- **Rules about what information can be made public and what cannot.** Without clear direction, someone will eventually post information about the organization that's searchable. Someone else will find it, and that could be the press, competitors, or government regulators.

INDISCREET FRIENDING

A great example of why a policy can be valuable comes from a bank executive who recently found that mixing personal and professional contacts could be dangerous. Our executive works for a large banking services supplier, and was excited to open a Facebook account. Without any guidance from the organization, he connected with the three top customers of his company. He also friended his 20-year-old son.

Within two weeks, his son posted an expletive-filled screed and needless to say, offended said customers with both his language and political stance. A written company policy forbidding mixing customers and personal contacts on a social site would have avoided this embarrassing situation.

- **Rules for mixing or not mixing personal and professional contacts under one account.** It's critical to set clear guidelines on this topic. Without them, people may combine the personal with the professional in ways that harm the reputation of the organization.

- **Best practices for creating online content.** These are usually tips that guide people on the quality level, voice, and style of anything written that includes the name of the organization, or is written by someone representing the organization.

- **Rules for approval of online content that involves the organization's name.** In certain situations, it makes sense to have a second or third person sign off on any content that's posted on the organization's behalf.

- **Advice on handling negative online comments about the organization.** The last thing you want is a flame war between an employee and an unknown person posting content. Guidelines about how to handle negative comments help people know where to draw the line between being supportive and loyal, and looking like an adolescent defending his or her territory.

- **Advice on the tone of voice to use when speaking for the company.** One of the important new dynamics of social tech is the firm's option to create an organizational voice. In most cases, this voice has specific properties, and when people are speaking on behalf of the organization, they need to keep some level of consistency.

- **Rules on using your title and organization's name on your profile or as a signature on content produced.** This is an important area to cover for security reasons and for reputation considerations. You don't want people using titles and names if you need to keep a low profile, or the organization's reputation can be besmirched by employees writing unenlightened posts.

- **Rules or advice on what social tools are the best to use both inside and outside the organization.** This can be helpful for new people because it gives them a quick list of the tools they need to use or learn. It can also help drive standard usage of specific tools.

- **Information on the dangers of weak security practices.** Social technologies can provide a new, gaping hole for bad guys to get into the organization. It's smart to include information on what a good password is, what havoc giving out too much information can cause, and the danger of clicking on every link indiscretely.

- **Information on training programs.** If the organization provides any type of training, it's good to describe it in the policy document. It serves both as an alert for new people who need training and a statement to whoever may review the document that the organization does more than simply state rules.

Bad Guys Whenever you see us use the descriptor "bad guys," we are wrapping up a number of people who mean to do harm. This could be a hacker looking to be destructive to your Web site or data. It could be a competitor looking to steal critical **KEY TERM** information. It could also be an ex-employee who is looking for revenge. The most dangerous of all bad guys is actually a current employee who is looking to gain access to information he or she isn't supposed to have. These bad guys are dangerous because they often have access to some of the software applications in the organization already.

The Format Options for Policy Documents

There are two options as to the form of the policy document. The first is to create a one- or two-page overview of the more important rules and include this document with the standard employment forms and language provided by the HR department. The benefit of this is that it carries the weight of an employment document, and often gets reviewed because it's distributed with other critical rules and policies.

The second option is to create a 10- to 12-page policy that not only has the critical rules, but also adds several hints and samples that help people understand what's expected and forbidden. This document could contain the entire list of areas to cover that we listed above and this level of detail makes a clear statement of expectations.

Make sure you emphasize the fact that the implications of indiscreet use of social tools can not only be embarrassing, it can also open up the company to legal issues. An employee who says something publicly that should not have been disclosed is acting as your representative and what he or she says will be permanent, widespread, and expensive. This is especially true if you have no policy to point to so that you can show the employee at least broke the rules by what he or she did.

BETTER SAFE THAN SORRY

A smart manager decides what should go into a policy document by combining an understanding of the level of danger if someone is indiscreet with using social tools and the demographics of the organization. The more people you have on staff, the more you should lean toward a deep explanation of the rules and guidelines. The more legal ramifications you have if someone makes a mistake, the more you want an expansive document. For example, if you're publicly traded and leaking information could earn a huge fine, you should make sure employees are familiar with the longer version of the policy. A short document might be easier to facilitate, but will be worthless to you if it doesn't cover all the areas that could be dangerous to the organization.

When you're comfortable that you have the right document and content in place, be sure you review the information with all of your people. Many times documents are overlooked or merely scanned by employees. It's the manager's responsibility to assure that all employees are conversant with the policy.

Hopefully you're starting to see how important your role is in helping the organization integrate social technologies into the workplace. There really isn't an option for a manager to sit back and let this new movement happen without direction. Social tools from a management standpoint should be viewed just as software, computers, and the phone system always have been. It's a tool that needs to be managed so that it gets used efficiently, safely, and securely.

Manager's Checklist for Chapter 3

☑ Goals and expectations need to be clearly set in order to guide employees to success. A manager must create a clear path to enlightenment on employee use of social tech. Absent a conscious effort to help people move forward, they'll stay ignorant or progress at such different rates as to create chaos.

☑ A manager must be a great example of appropriate and productive use. Leading by example is one of the most important hallmarks of a good leader. This truism certainly applies to social tech.

☑ A strong manager has a process for onboarding new employees and teaching them social tech best practices. Getting people off on the right foot has many benefits. Don't miss the chance to use social tools to speed up the integration process for new hires.

☑ Managers can put extra emphasis on *productive* social tech use by adding it to employee reviews. "What gets measured gets done" is a management truism.

☑ Don't use social tools as a replacement for a face-to-face discussion (even if over video) when providing negative feedback or counseling to employees. While they need to show a good example of social tech use, managers need to be careful of overusing it and attempting to lead people by managing over the wire, when a face-to-face meeting would be more appropriate.

☑ Written guidelines and policies are crucial for directing proper use and protecting the organization. This is a step that can't be skipped. Employees need written guidelines, and managers need to ensure that employees understand and follow the guidelines.

Chapter
4

Managing the Use
of Social Tools

A critical talent that you should develop is the ability to evaluate an employee's skills in effective use of social tools. Depending on the position for which you're hiring, social tech skills might be more or less important.

For the jobs that can be heavily augmented by applying social tools, the quality of the work a person produces in the near future could vary by 50 percent when using social tools well—or not. The difficult thing about this is we don't have much history in knowing how to "grade" a person's social tech skills.

When interviewing a prospective employee, there are a number of questions you can ask that could provide a quick picture of the person's proficiency. For example:

- How many friends, followers, or contacts do you have online?
- How often do you post information online?
- What applications do you use regularly?
- Do you create content for sites like YouTube, SlideShare, Flickr, or Scribd?
- When you need to find a solution to a problem, do you ever use your online network? Give me an example of when you did this.
- Have you ever started an eCommunity? Describe it to me.
- How do you find out about new social tech features and applications?

The answers to these questions will give you a good idea of an applicant's proficiency with social tools. Of course another easy thing you can do is run a few Internet searches through sites like Google, Socialmention, and Addictomatic to see how socially relevant the person is. This is easier to do if the person has an unusual name. For the people who have names like "John Smith" you need to add a few search terms to delineate the John Smith you're trying to locate. In this case, it's also a good idea to ask the person for his or her specific usernames on social sites so you can track him or her down more easily.

Does the thought of asking someone for his or her usernames make you a bit uneasy? This won't be that farfetched in the near future because we're moving now toward using these tools in our career, so they become another way to check our credentials.

SMART   **UNDERSTANDING SEARCHABILITY**

MANAGING

There is no way to monitor or understand the state of your online reputation if you can't figure out where the content is that mentions you or the organization. It's dangerous to just accept that mentions cannot be found because you have a common name. A new technique people are using is to standardize on a unique username that can be tracked more easily. So if your name is John Smith, go with a username of JSmithOkla (if you live in Oklahoma). This is unique enough to isolate mentions of you specifically.

What Are the Boundaries of Privacy?

Because social tools started off as something that people used personally, there are many who feel it's an invasion of privacy to have an organization snooping in their online properties. The motivation behind tracking someone online is purely to determine a person's proficiency with social tools, but obviously HR departments have been running searches on people applying for jobs for years. At this point, it's no longer an invasion of privacy if a person is willingly posting information to a public social site. Whatever the company can find online, other employees, competitors, and customers can also find, so it's relevant to a potential employer.

As time goes on, skills such as learning how to manage one's online reputation, the ability to leverage crowdsourcing to get work done, the

> ### Social Tech and the Interview Process
>
> **CAUTION**
>
> Online information posted by an applicant or someone who knows the applicant can be a valuable glimpse into areas you would never get to in an interview. Be careful about overreacting to what you might find. As social sites get more pervasive and information is stored for a long time, you're going to run into items that might speak to maturity levels that have long since changed. Everyone has a personal life, and many people have made mistakes in judgment. You might pass on a star employee needlessly if you overreact to something you find.

ability to build a powerful river of information into one's brain, and the ability to leverage a network of friends and associates to answer questions and find resources are going to be more and more valuable. A smart manager is able to assess someone's abilities and map ways to improve weak areas through training and guidance.

Social Tech and Personality Types

Another consideration to take into account when evaluating a person's social tech skill, or potential ability to add skills, is personality type. There has been little research done on personality types and the proclivity to adapt to social tools, but some basic assumptions can be made. For example, it's only natural that an introvert and an extrovert might view the concept of eCommunity differently. An extrovert will naturally be interested in online discussions, conversations, and relating to people through online tools. An introvert will be less apt to want to participate in a group or community-based activities.

The important aspect to note about personality traits is how they might impact what people are more or less likely to be drawn to, and how that might influence how you manage them. Let's take a look at a few other personality traits and see how they might show up.

> ### Judging Personality Types as Good or Bad
>
> **CAUTION**
>
> Be careful not to assume that a person of a specific personality type will be good or bad with social tools. Someone who may not be good in one facet might be outstanding in other areas. For example, an introvert might not be great with online conversations, but could be tremendous at producing and sharing valuable content and research pieces.

Very aggressive, rugged individualistic, type "A" personalities may dislike the thought of having to learn a whole new way of doing things because they are busy with their current lists. In addition, they might see little value in connecting with others unless they see a specific need. Their communication style when they reach out to others may be in short bursts. The thought of writing a page or two of blog posts every week may seem daunting on top of their regular jobs. The bottom line is they feel they have little time for this in some cases, and when they do use the tools, it's only to give a short answer or to lurk on conversations to see what others are doing.

KEY TERM **Lurking** This term refers to a person who participates in a social site or conversation only as a listener. The person does not offer observations or provide opinions or content. He or she is simply watching what other people are doing.

Artistic and creative people often enjoy connecting with others, sharing ideas, and getting inspired by communicating with people in their field. They'll enjoy creating content and sharing it on social media sites, and browsing through content others have created. They usually don't feel pressured and make time to learn how to use social tools because they see it as a critical part of their careers. They love the idea that social media provide a huge playground of potential material and examples. Social tech is one big leap forward in their ability to do what they enjoy.

Detailed accounting-type personalities may enjoy the aspects that let them build rivers of information on the subjects they deal with. They like the capability of searching for people and learning about them online (mostly for security or ethics reasons). They may not be as interested in connecting with people socially, but are fine with connecting with contacts at a professional level.

Empathetic/sensitive personality styles have a mixed mind concerning social tools. They like being involved in lots of conversations, sharing how they feel with lots of people at once, and staying up on how others are doing. They enjoy passing around feel-good stories and content they run across, and often see these tools as a vehicle to help others feel good. They dislike that they have to relate to a machine instead of a warm-blooded human when communicating because they feel so much is lost by not being there in person. They love the face-to-face communication paths.

These are all generalizations, of course, and are simply meant to make you aware that people adapt to social tech in different ways. You'll run into people who seem to fight the whole notion of social tech, people who use a single area, or people who are addicted to using it for several hours a day. Much of this is driven by personality type, and until people who are not naturally inclined to use a tool like this see value in areas they relate to, they'll leave these tools in the toolbox.

DIFFERENCES ON THE EXECUTIVE TEAM

FOR EXAMPLE

The executive team at a fast-growing entrepreneurial firm is a good example. The CEO is an old pro who has seen it all. He believes social tech is a huge time waster, and would rather spend his time shaking hands and playing golf with bankers and potential customers. The head of marketing is deep into all forms of social tools and has been successful at finding high-quality leads for the sales team through her skills. The CFO uses social tools to keep up on changes at the IRS, industry regulations, and to communicate with investors. His use must always be based on cost or labor efficiency.

Appropriate Use of Social Tools

This leads us to defining the appropriate use of social tools at work. This might seem like a simple area because the logical answer to this is that the use is appropriate if it concerns work, and is among and between people who are coworkers, customers, or business partners. Unfortunately, it isn't that simple.

In the old days, businesspeople documented their "network" of contacts with a Rolodex or binder full of business cards. This collection was critical to their success because it represented the hard-earned fruits of years of meeting people through social events and business transactions. For the most part, everyone in his or her network had been met in person somewhere along the way. Some people were better than others at keeping their documentation and information up to date. When changing jobs it was common to lose contact with much of one's network. This included losing touch with most of the people he or she had worked with previously.

We progressed to software-based contact management systems. They allowed us to archive our contacts electronically on the organization's computers and in some ways that provided benefits; however, one huge drawback was that when a person changed jobs, he or she often lost all of his or her contacts if the company was unwilling to let him or her have an electronic copy of the contacts database. Some employees were smart enough to keep an offline copy, but in many cases, their network shrank by 90 percent when they walked out the door.

The world is a different place now because our contacts are saved in systems like LinkedIn and Plaxo and they now update automatically when someone changes any aspect of his or her career. These systems even push pictures and the full contact database right to our mobile devices so we always have the latest information without doing the updating ourselves. Better yet, when we leave an organization, we still own our contacts because we own the accounts that archive them.

Even better, we have the awesome ability to connect with people whom we never meet in person. We connect with them strictly because they have a shared interest, or maybe they share a contact with us. We even have the ability to access all the contacts of our contacts, which means we can tap into thousands of people we don't even know. The Rolodex never gave us that. If you think about it, we have progressed in unbelievable ways with how we nurture and use our network of contacts from a mere 15 years ago. And this is where the problems start for appropriate social tech use at work.

SMART MANAGING

THE OWNERSHIP OF CONTACT INFORMATION

An area of concern that you must deal with is who "owns" the contacts that an employee generates while employed. For organizations that have customer relationship management (CRM) software, all contacts should be entered into that system. But is it OK for employees to also connect to all these contacts through social tools like Plaxo so they can use them when they leave the company? What about the employees' business contacts that they bring to the company when employed? Should they be required to enter them in the CRM system? A manager makes a conscious decision about who owns contacts and what access is given when employment is terminated.

The Difficulty Discerning Personal and Professional Contacts

There's no question that people shouldn't have personal conversations using social tools during work hours or read personal content. This is no different than the rules we've always had for phone use. They should not be viewing nonwork-related videos on YouTube any more than they should be in the breakroom watching TV. Those are obvious lines to draw.

But what about nurturing relationships with people who might be useful from a business standpoint? What about using your Facebook friends to find needed resources? What about reading Twitter streams from people who are thought leaders in your field of work? What about sending updates out to your network about what you are working on at the moment in case someone has something helpful to share? It all gets a little fuzzy, especially when a friend is also a possible business contact in the future!

We have to acknowledge that the generation coming into the workforce now is being raised using online collaboration tools, building large online networks, and using them to help solve problems, or simply help each other out. *The relationship with their online community is something that people who have not worked in this way won't understand.* The comment you hear from someone who doesn't participate in the social tech world is the following: "These young people just sit around texting and playing on Facebook all day." In some cases that might be true. In other cases, they are nurturing a network that they leverage in powerful ways to get their jobs done.

This creates a dilemma for a manager. Do you literally have to look over a person's shoulder every time he or she brings up a social site to see if the person is using it valuably or not? Maybe just blocking social tech usage altogether is simpler. As discussed earlier, this is a poor option for many positions in an organization because they need social tools to communicate with vendors, customers, and partners. The dynamics of how the next generation will operate, and how many older people must move to, include an immense amount of attention being paid to one's electronic network. Not because it's a plaything, but because it's a new way to get things done. Managing people who are leveraging these tools or abusing them is going to be difficult, because discerning what they are doing when they are interfacing with a screen will be impossible. The solution to managing effectively in this environment lies in a direction that will make some managers uncomfortable, but is likely to be where we end up, like it or not.

The Secret Formula for Driving Appropriate Use

There is a simple, two-part solution to assuring appropriate use of social tools. The first is to use software that monitors time spent on sites. This only works if you have an IT department that can implement monitoring systems and provide the reports to you. It also depends on your employees using the company computer to use the social sites instead of their mobile devices. *If* you can monitor usage and *if* people use the company computer, you can find out if someone is spending too much time online in the wrong sites. It won't tell you if the person is doing something valuable in the right sites. These usage reports will at least give you a place to start if there is a potential problem.

The second solution is the more likely to take hold in the future, and that is to move people who have access to social tools at work to more performance-based pay schemas. In this scenario, you stipulate what's required to get the job done or to exceed expectations, provide the possible pay-per-performance measurements, and let them use technology tools any way they choose. If they are great with leveraging social tech as a tool, and everything else is solid with their skills and work ethic, they'll perform well. If they abuse these tools and/or have no skills or work ethic, they won't perform well, and the results will be telling.

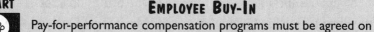

SMART **EMPLOYEE BUY-IN**

MANAGING

Pay-for-performance compensation programs must be agreed on by both parties. A smart manager won't design a performance-based pay program without input from employees. When transitioning people from a fixed salary model to something with a performance pay component, some people worry that this is a way to lower their pay. Make sure that people see this as a way to position themselves to make more money by providing outstanding value, instead of as a way to make less money. The most effective pay models align the goals of the organization with those of the employee.

It's Only Going to Get More Complicated!

If this sounds radical that things are going to get even more complicated, think about this. As time goes on, there will be more and more people using social tools. There will be more devices to access them. There will be more mixing of personal and professional contacts and communications. And now with location-based tools like Foursquare and Google Latitude, we're mixing into the equation where people are physically located!

We can't stop the tide of socially augmented workplaces, so what other solution is there? We can't tear apart personal use from professional because they're inexorably entwined. Performance-based pay models are a result of getting to a place where we say to people, "We can't govern how you use technology tools, nor the hours you choose to work, so we'll measure you on results produced and not time spent at work, or how you get it done."

This is an obvious step that comes when you transition from a manufacturing economy where you can watch people work with their hands and measure their output easily to the knowledge economy. When the majority of jobs are done by interfacing with a computer screen, we have to give up thinking we can oversee every minute of technology usage and measure the results.

So at the end of the day, what's the definition of appropriate use? How about this: appropriate use is time invested using social tools that has a direct benefit for the organization either through nurturing contacts that are useful in problem-solving, resource-gathering, or lead generation (e.g., LinkedIn, Facebook, Plaxo, Jigsaw, Spoke). Or, any use of social tools for business that lowers the costs of communicating or increases the speed of information exchange (e.g., Skype, Twitter messaging). In addition, any use that provides content to improve the quality of information flow to the users so they have an improved ability to perform their duties (blogs, RSS feeds, SlideShare, Scribd).

Best Practices for Managing the Posting of Online Information

Another new talent you need going forward is the ability to help employees understand the best practices and safe habits for posting information online. Many people don't understand the repercussions of what they post online. Once you click that Send button, your words, pictures, videos, or presentations are now permanently on some servers and out of your control. This information is likely searchable by any word contained in what you posted and can be read by virtually anyone on the Web. This has serious repercussions for organizations as more people begin to use *their own discretion* on what they say about the organization publicly.

For this reason, managers need to step into the breach and help employees understand what is appropriate to discuss online when talking about the organization or while posting using their employee job title. We're already seeing many painful stories of people who, without thinking, posted information or content that came back to haunt both them and the organization. Let's look at a few examples of mistakes people have made:

- A young person attending a meeting at a publicly traded company hears a comment about sales being off by a large percentage this quarter and repeats the conversation to friends on Facebook. The press picks up this post on an alert they run on the company and goes public with a comment that was meant to be internal.
- A well-meaning salesperson responds to comments made by a competitor on a blog with incorrect information that becomes embarrassing when it's used by the competitor as evidence that the company is out of touch.
- A not-so-well-meaning salesperson flames a competitor on a well-read blog site while using a pseudo-identity and is found out. The resulting press is embarrassing for his company.
- A flight attendant for a major airline posts sexually provocative pictures of herself in her uniform. Another employee notifies the HR department. This leads to termination and embarrassment for the company when the story goes public in the mainstream press.
- A high-level engineer for a large software company announces on a blog that a new platform will be coming out soon, and the blog is riddled with spelling errors. The press sees this as a metaphor for the quality of the soon-to-be-released product.

- An employee of another software company posts what he thinks is a funny video of the executive team playing as an ad hoc band at a company party. The video goes viral and is ridiculed by people as an immature act by leadership.

- An employee tweets about how much she hates working with one of her customers. She goes into detail about how difficult

> **ONLINE DAMAGE CONTROL**
> **SMART**
> **MANAGING**
>
> How an organization handles a negative-content event is important. There's no sense making something go viral by adding to the online discussion, or exacerbating the problem by trying to defend something negative. It's best to provide a public mea culpa on behalf of the person posting and/or the organization. People are forgiving when you admit a mistake. When employees use bad judgment, counsel them first, have them pull the content if possible, and use the incident as a teaching moment for everyone else.

it is to deal with a specific person on the customer's staff. Of course the company runs a listening program on their name and in minutes has forwarded copies to the CEO's office. The employee had no idea that anyone would see what she thought went out only to her handful of followers.

- An employee finds an unflattering picture of the CEO and forwards it to all his friends online, and then saves it on his Flickr account. He proceeds to enter the CEO's name as a keyword and now every time someone searches on the CEO's name, the picture comes up in the search.

Of course this list can go on, and we are only a few years into the ability to upload content to the collective Internet. Imagine the repercussions of things like this when we have twice as many people using the Internet, five times as many people using social tools, and every competitor running alert programs for any mention of your organization's name.

What You Can Do to Avoid Embarrassing Postings

Let's look at a few best practices that give you at least a fighting chance to avoid inappropriate content going public and the legal issues that can arise from these kinds of indiscretions. In many ways, we have handed people a tool that is more powerful than they realize. The first line of defense is training. Everyone who has access to a computer must be trained on how content exists on the Web, and the potential dangers. This includes training people on any regulations that the company might be under, due to being publicly traded or in a regulated space like the finance industry.

Another good practice is for a manager to approve all content that is going to be posted. This includes anything posted on behalf of the company, or anything an employee is going to post using his or her job title. This slows things down and creates a layer of bureaucracy, but it also can save people from themselves.

The last line of defense is to include all the rules and helpful hints for content posting in the social tech governance policy. This not only makes it clear to everyone what the rules are, it also adds the weight of a possible termination if the rules are broken. This normally causes people to pause a few seconds before posting content.

Building Acceptable and Effective Online Profiles

One of the basic aspects of using social tools is the obligatory profile that every site provides. This area is a hidden danger from a few aspects. When people first sign up with social sites, they typically either input the minimum information required to open an account, or they take the time to complete every field of information requested. Much like posting content, many people give little thought as to the impact a profile can have on their lives, careers, or safety.

The first fact to understand about a profile is that it's searchable. Not only that, a few of the social sites (Facebook, Twitter, and LinkedIn) actually help Google index their profiles so that people can more easily find you. So it's a fallacy to think you can have a personal site separate from your career site. Unless you use a completely different name in your profile, anyone with whom you do business can find your personal site sitting right next to your professional presence. Of course this means that anything you say or any picture you upload on your personal site will be seen by all.

What does that mean? It means that if you say that you are single and provide the city you live in, anyone who wants to do one search further can figure out exactly where you live. Post a glamour shot of yourself in a sexy pose, and now you've advertised something to people you might not have wished to advertise. This is one example of what can become a safety issue with indiscrete profile handling. Of less danger personally, but potentially embarrassing professionally, can be the lists of information that social sites love for you to fill out, such as music tastes, favorite movies, favorite foods, political party, etc., etc., etc.

Let's be clear, social sites want more information all the time, and it's not for the benefit of the user. It's because sites make money by selling our information to advertisers so they can more precisely target potential customers. This makes sense and may be a fair trade-off for getting to use these social services for free. The problem with this whole scenario is the potential for people to post what they think is OK in their personal lives, only to find out that every coworker and client can see this information.

When helping employees learn how to build professional, acceptable profiles, you may find problems at both ends of the spectrum. On one side will be people who provide too much information, and some of that may be inappropriate if business partners or competitors find it. At the other end of the spectrum are the people who enter name, rank, and serial number only, and this could be a negative when trying to facilitate new business relationships. Finding that appropriate and productive middle ground is a skill that all professional people are going to need to find.

> **THE PROFILE SCREENSHOT**
> **SMART**
> **MANAGING**
>
> A powerful training aid is for a manager to search on social sites for a handful of their employees' profiles, screen capture the information, and put it into a PowerPoint presentation. Be careful not to grab a profile that has anything that will overly embarrass someone. At the appropriate time, bring up the screenshots of the profiles and review what they say, and see if anyone believes they should improve, delete, or change any of the content.

Social Tech and Security Issues

Social technologies have created a whole world of negative side effects for IT departments, because the technologies expose the organization to hackers and malware. This single danger has been enough for many organizations to block social sites completely. There are two open doors that have been created for the bad guys. The first is simply more ways to get ignorant users to click on links they should leave alone. The second is holes in the software applications themselves that let bad guys use poorly built social applications to access company assets.

Malware Describes any small bit of code that can be injected into a device **KEY TERM** or network with harmful intent. This includes viruses, keyboard loggers, zombie controls, and spambots.

By the very nature of social sites, users connect with people they may or may not know. Users don't know for sure that the person on the other end of the communication is who they think they are. There is a growing flood of postings and communications to wade through every day so people don't always pay close attention to the signs that they are being attacked or socially engineered.

The Fallacy of Depending on Users to Be Security-Conscious

The reality about security is that even a great IT department can't stop users from clicking on something they shouldn't, or answering a question they should ignore. The best thing an organization can do is to provide regular training to update users on the latest exploits that bad guys are using. Once people are trained, they more often make good decisions.

Unfortunately, many organizations assume that users make good decisions around security all on their own. In many cases they don't. You

Social Engineering Refers to a bad guy using a bag of tricks to get a user to take an action or answer a question he or she should not. This term actually predates the term "social **KEY TERM** tech," and was coined years ago in the security space. The word "social" in this social engineering context refers to a person using a conversation, question, or contact using false information to get what he or she wants. For example, sending someone a message saying that his or her e-mail account is broken and not delivering all the mail and asking for the username and password so that the mail can be properly delivered. Naïve people sometimes give this information out because they think if someone asks the question, they must be honest. In reality, the user has been socially engineered.

can play a valuable role by ensuring that your employees at least get some training from someone with a technology-based security background. At minimum, you should highlight this as an issue every now and then.

A powerful learning experience for employees is how a manager handles a security event when one arises. When people make bad decisions concerning security and must have their machines cleaned of viruses, or when they lose control of their social tech site because they were socially engineered, the manager has been presented with a learning experience for everyone. Instead of sweeping something like this under the rug, it's good to mention it at a staff meeting. Point out that the social tech world is still a dangerous thing if users aren't diligent about what they are doing, with whom they are communicating, or what they are clicking on.

When considering everything discussed in this section, it should be obvious that a manager must consistently keep an eye on what people are doing with social tools. You can't, for weeks at a time, take your eye off how these tools are being used. These tools have a huge potential to benefit or injure an organization, and the outcome is often dictated by the diligence you provide in leading people in productive directions.

Manager's Checklist for Chapter 4

☑ It's critical to evaluate employees' or applicants' proficiency with social tools. This helps you know what unique skills can be leveraged, or what needs improvement so a plan can be put together.

☑ Personality types will adapt to various social tech tools differently, and you must account for this. In some cases, personality styles will be a barrier from people using social tools.

☑ What people post online is forever, a representation of them, and can enhance or damage their careers. It can also become a legal issue for the organization, or at minimum, embarrassing. A good manager will help employees be aware of this and provide education that helps avoid negative incidents.

☑ It's necessary to be able to discern beneficial use of these tools while someone is at work. It's possible for a heavy user to be online a good amount of time and still be productive. Or, he or she might be wasting company time. You should be able to discern the difference and motivate people by focusing on results and not how people are using the tools.

☑ Social tools are causing problems for IT departments because it's a whole new open door for bad guys. Managers must be on top of this and help their people.

☑ Social tech use is not an area that a manager can ignore for weeks at a time. It can be a powerful tool or a huge distraction. Most times the manager is the difference in which it will be.

Selecting the Best Social Tech Tools

One aspect of managing social tech that's more difficult than dealing with other business tools is the explosion of possibilities in the applications that you can put to use. There simply is no comparison with any time in history when it comes to the speed at which new social tools are coming into being, penetrating the workforce, and in some cases, disappearing. A number of interesting dynamics are driving this and we should take a look at what's behind this veritable bounty.

Easy Construction

The first dynamic driving the current torrent of new applications is the ease with which developers can write software and release it to the public. In many cases, the capabilities offered to us aren't complicated, and therefore, not that difficult to construct. Twitter is a good example because when it was first built it was a simple idea, and a fairly easy piece of software to write. It certainly got more complicated as millions started to use it, and as new ideas for functionality cropped up.

Add this ease of development to ease of delivery to millions of users with the touch of a button, and you have a formula for tons of people trying to get in the game as developers. Just stop and think for a second about how easy it is to deliver one of these Web-based applications—no

> ### THE FIRE HOSE IS TURNED ON!
> It's no exaggeration to say that there is literally a new social tech tool coming onto the Internet daily. If you care to go online and visit the techcrunch.com blog on any given day, odds are high you'll see a new social tech application being announced. TechCrunch is a great source for information on what is happening in this field. So even if today happens to be that rare day that something new isn't announced, you'll at least be able to add a valuable resource if you are not reading it already.

advertising, no sales team, no documentation, no customer service organization, etc. Add all of these benefits to the fame that comes to the developer who escalates his or her status from unknown cube-dwelling coder to a technology superstar. It's easy to see why it's so attractive to mix a clever idea with a few hundred hours of programming and the Web as a delivery vehicle, and see what you get on the market.

Social Tech Platforms

There is another factor driving this innovation explosion. Companies like Facebook, Google, and Twitter have developed their underlying capabilities into platforms that allow for third parties to write applications on top of their systems. Each has "opened" their platforms and hundreds of developers have rushed in to build products that embed, use, or extend their functionality. This is helpful to platform providers because it creates more demand for their platform and gives it extended capabilities that the platform provider didn't have to build. At the end of the day, the platform provider gets to own the access to the users, and the ability to advertise to them, as well.

>
> ### THE TWITTER ECOSYSTEM
> **TOOLS** Twitter as a platform provides an interesting look into how platforms and the tools that use them may blossom in the future. Twitter also demonstrates what can be difficult when choosing and managing the tools an organization may want to standardize on. For example, most people sign up for Twitter to get an account name and then never go back to their site. They'll use tools like Tweetdeck.com, Twellow.com, Listorious.com, Hootsuite.com, Klout.com, or Cotweet.com to manage their use of Twitter. None of these tools were produced by Twitter, yet all of them extend the value of the base platform.

How About This for a Good Price—FREE

Another factor driving the proliferation of social tools is the price. Let's be honest, when we don't have to pay for a new tool, the decision to download it or sign up for it is pretty simple. If it has *any* chance of being something of value to us, we'll try it out. For this reason, the sales job of people who have a new idea for an application is pretty easy. They don't face a price barrier so they're more than happy to take a risk on an idea by writing the application in their spare time, putting it out on the Web, and seeing what happens. If millions of people use it, they can find a revenue model in there somewhere. Even if they don't, the street credibility of being the developer who provides a tool that millions of people use could land them a serious salary at one of the larger tech companies, and odds are someone will buy the rights to the application for a good price.

Social Tool Developers (At Times) Hit the Jackpot!

This leads to the final dynamic that's driving the volume of social tools onto the market: the rewards developers can get from building a well-received application. Of course there are the stories of the mega successful people like the founders of Google, YouTube, Facebook, etc. People who developed their companies while in their early 20s and were obscenely wealthy by their late 20s. Setting those aside, there are many more you've not heard of who built companies and sold them upstream for a handful of millions. Not a bad payday for a few years of hard work. With the real possibility of a new social tech application being a lottery ticket, the money becomes a powerful driver of innovation—and volume of applications.

THE DANGERS OF FREE

Although being able to download lots of cool social tools for free sounds like a winner all the way around, there are pitfalls. The first is that without a price barrier, employees have no reason not to download and try out every new thing they run across. This can be a security problem and hurts your ability to standardize tools.

The other problem is that there are times when paying a little bit to get an enterprise-class tool would be a better idea than using a lightweight application. Make sure you're aware of the possibility of a premium version of a tool you're using heavily because, for a small subscription fee, you could be making a better decision.

THE DIFFERENCE IN LISTENING TOOLS

FOR EXAMPLE

A great example of the quality in social tools can be found in the category of listening applications. These are tools that monitor all the social tech information streams online and notify you of any use of your name (or the organization's name). There are many free tools out there, and some that you pay for. If you use a free tool that finds 25% of the mentions of your name, versus an application you pay for that would find 90% of the mentions, you're being penny wise and pound foolish.

Combine the money with developers' natural desire to turn their ideas into reality, and you have thousands of smart people experimenting in this field.

The Role of the Manager and Social Tools

All of this leads to a dilemma for you because someone has to try out and coordinate or standardize the social tech tools used in the organization. Failure to manage and coordinate what tools are used leads to chaos in the organization over time as everyone uses his or her preferred services. Worse yet, you may be faced with people who aren't even aware of critical tools they *could* be using that would be beneficial. The productivity difference between using a basic social tool and an advanced application can be dramatic.

Don't Panic, You Can Learn to Be an Expert

If you're overwhelmed with the thought that you might need to be the social tool cop when you can barely use social tools personally, relax. This is a great time to get help from the more technology-savvy people you manage. It's not critical that you know the benefits of every social tool in detail. It's just important for you to be aware of what your people are using, and new applications

---

SMART MANAGING

THE STARTER LIST

A simple thing you can do to help new employees get up to speed quickly is to maintain a list of the social tools the team uses. When new people come on board, provide the list to them and let them know that other employees use this list of applications. This lets the new hires know they can reach out to coworkers to get trained informally, and the capabilities that others around them will have.

that are coming into the organization from your early adopters. To the extent that you can see a specific tool winning heavy favor with your team, get the rest of the team to standardize on it. The tougher task is when there's no clear winner and you see the team using different tools to accomplish the same tasks.

Choosing the Best Applications

As mentioned, the functionality difference between a good and average application can be huge. Add to that the chaos that's caused if you chase the latest new features that don't make up for the lack of standardization, and you have some tough decisions on which applications to use in-house. Yet, it's your job to play a roll in picking the applications your people should use. You're the one who needs to have the institutional knowledge as to what social tools best help your people accomplish what they need to do. New people depend on you to tell them which tools to use. Current staff appreciate your ability to recommend the applications that are the easiest, most functional to use. You probably never thought you'd play this kind of role. Welcome to the "Social Century."

So how does one choose the best applications? The easiest way to answer this is to give you another set of bullet points to use to filter through the many applications here today and coming soon. These are in no particular order, and all are critical in making wise decisions.

- **Functionality.** This is a simple filter. Does the application do something valuable that will improve the way a task is done today, or provide a completely new capability?
- **Ease of use (ease of learning).** Functionality isn't as exciting if no one can figure out how to use an application. It's helpful if applications are intuitive, have a well-designed user interface, and are easy to learn without formal training.
- **Constituent use.** In some cases, it makes sense to standardize on an application because it's what your customer base is already using. This filter could also apply if your employees have all been using a specific application at home on their personal machines. If your constituents are generally using Facebook as an eCommunity, it doesn't make much sense to force them to work on MySpace.

- **Strategic considerations.** Sometimes the choice of tool has a lot to do with what your competition uses, or what will create the right image for your organization. If your organization has an image as a trend-setter, you may want to experiment with new platforms. If you're more conservative, stick with the most widely used options.

- **Budget.** In a world where there are many free tools and lots of cost-cutting, budget can often be a go/no go filter. It often makes sense to use a free version of a tool, and later move to a paid subscription version when you're sure you can leverage the capabilities and provide a good return on investment.

- **Data standards.** It's increasingly important to assure that every piece of software you use can connect to the organization's digital plumbing. Unless the social tool is completely stand-alone, you must make sure the data generated can be easily moved in and out of the current IT infrastructure.

- **General public acceptance.** Depending on the classification of tools you're thinking of using, the volume of people already using it makes a difference. For example, there isn't much use in a crowdsourcing tool that has a very small crowd supplying the services. It's hard to justify moving to an eCommunity site if there are almost no people in the community. Twitter would not be very valuable if only a few people were tweeting.

- **Security.** This is a filter too many people ignore. Not because they don't care, but because they don't imagine there could be a security issue. You can't make decisions on functionality alone without considering the open doors you might create with a new application.

SMART

MANAGING

ASK FOR HELP FROM AN IT EXPERT

When it comes to understanding computer security, take this advice: sit down with a technology person who is knowledgeable about security and get some instruction on the dangers of social technologies. If you're willing to invest a little time getting training on how malware or bad guys use social tech as an open door into your systems, you'd be surprised how clear the picture will become. You'll learn new vocabulary and security concepts that will allow you to explain in detail why discretion must be used when handling social tech applications.

This is a great time to ask for counsel from an IT department person and improve your general security knowledge.

■ **Privacy.** The nature of social tools is that they help people connect and share information. This opens up issues with privacy. Make sure you understand where the text goes that your people type on the screen, who has access to it, and how easy it might be to block it from the public. Note that Facebook has more than 170 combinations of privacy settings, and this is due to the importance of the issue. There is organizational information you don't want shared publicly, so be sure that the applications you choose can prevent prying eyes from snooping in on your conversations.

OUTSOURCING DECISIONS

Be careful about giving in to a desire to outsource these decisions to a member of the team who seems to be fluent in the social space. If you lack personal knowledge of social tools, it's worth making the investment in getting up to speed. Managers who assign others to make decisions they should make find that when problems occur, they'll be stuck having to admit they didn't understand what was being granted when they handed permission over to someone else.

CAUTION

Categories of Social Tools Available

Keep in mind there are various types of tools, and it might be wise to put more emphasis on some areas over others when you have a limited time to invest in choosing your standard applications. Most organizations of any size are already using one or more applications in each of the categories listed below. As you read through this list, think about what you're using and where it fits. This is a basic list and isn't meant to be comprehensive. Even within this list, see if there are categories that you are completely missing at this point.

■ **Communication tools.** These tools include anything specifically provided to enhance social networking or communications internally. Examples are Blogger, Wordpress, Skype, Yammer, or Twitter.

■ **eCommunity tools.** These tools help groups of people congregate in virtual walled gardens. They typically help people find like-minded contacts or others with shared interests. These include Facebook, MySpace, LinkedIn, and Ning.

- **Social media management tools.** Applications like Radian6, Viralheat, SM2 (by Alterian), Hootsuite, and Spredfast help organizations manage specific social media campaigns, measure the positive versus negative comments made online, and coordinate the delivery of information through multiple social sources.
- **Aggregation tools.** With so much information and content flying around the social sphere, it's important to use tools that help aggregate all this information into one screen. Tools like Tweetdeck, Hootsuite, Google Reader, and Netvibes are useful in coordinating lots of content into a simple view.
- **Listening tools.** To learn of mentions of your name in social spheres, tools like Addictomatic, Alerts.com, GoogleAlerts, Socialmention alerts, and Yotify can be used to notify you via e-mails. These tools are becoming critical in providing customer support and in doing ad hoc market research.
- **Research tools.** There are applications specifically designed to help you find information by leveraging the power of social contacts. For example, Spoke, Jigsaw, Yahoo, and Answers all take slightly different approaches to helping find an answer you might need.
- **Measurement tools.** One of the most-asked questions by people unfamiliar with social tool usage at work is "How do you measure if you're doing well with social tech?" Socialmention, Klout, and Twittalyzer are examples of applications that measure online relevancy so that you can be aware of your growing or shrinking influence online.
- **Crowdsourcing tools.** There are more than 75 sites dedicated to helping with crowdsourcing specific types of work. This varies from sites that facilitate problem solving to performing creative design and providing free market research. There are new sites being formed every month, and each one further targets a specific niche.
- **Social media sites.** YouTube, Scribd, Flickr, and SlideShare are examples most people are familiar with, and there are hundreds more. Just in the video space there are social media sites verticalizing video delivery. For example, Hulu for delivering TV content, or GodTube for delivering Christian social content.

Don't let this list overwhelm you. In most cases you will put much

AN EXAMPLE OF SOCIAL TOOL USAGE

Crowdsourcing can be used as an example of a powerful concept that helps you choose the appropriate tools. There are at least 75 sites that provide assistance with crowdsourcing, and many of them are specific to the task that needs to be done. There are also differing rules among the sites as to how a project gets presented to the crowd and great variation in the number of workers available. For these reasons, it's critical to not only know when you can use crowdsourcing as a tool, but also which site is the best one for the task.

more emphasis on communication, social media, and eCommunity tools than any other area. The rest of the tools are usually put into place once and then monitored. This means you can concentrate the time you have in tool management in just a few areas, so you can understand the best options for your team.

Dealing with Employees Who Prefer to Use Their Personal Applications

One last thought on choosing the best social applications for your team. A common situation that arises is that people will bring to work what they use at home. This can be a distraction or a positive, depending on how it's handled. The good news is you have someone who is using a social tech tool at home, has already learned it, and probably made lots of connections. Even better news, he has done this on his own time without your having to pay him! To the extent that he can use this tool at work, you have just gained extra value from this employee.

The negative is that once people get comfortable with a tool, they often don't want to give it up. The decision on whether to make someone standardize on a tool that you recommend versus one they have already made a time investment in can be dicey. This problem is likely to get more common as people invest more time into the use of a specific tool in their personal lives, and are less willing to switch to a tool the organization is promoting. As the leader, you often have to play Solomon and decide whether making someone change what she is using is worth the resistance you'll get. Standard applications are a good thing, yet when standardization keeps people from using the tools at all, you might be taking a step backwards.

> **TWEETDECK VERSUS HOOTSUITE**
>
> These two applications were both born out of the need to manage Twitter better than was provided in its Web site. As the need to post comments across various platforms grew, both applications added the ability to post across them with one entry. Then they began to allow the user to monitor various platforms all from one screen. At the moment, both are moving away from being known as a Twitter tool to being an aggregation tool. Both are good applications that get the job done. If users have already done the work to set one up, it wouldn't make sense to make them change to your choice when the solutions are so similar.

The trend we are now seeing with employees learning about social tools from their friends first, and then migrating them into their professional lives is something a bit new. From a management standpoint, there is nothing to fear from this new dynamic. We do have to be aware that it exists, and look to accentuate the positives by thinking of it as a grassroots form of R&D. We also must mitigate the negatives by making sure social application use does not become a free-for-all within the team.

Training Your Team Members

Training is one of the most beneficial investments you can make in the area of social tech—and yet it's virtually nonexistent in most organizations. While social tech is a powerful set of tools, and more people are trying them out every day, there are still many who don't know how to use them. Maybe we believe that people will magically assimilate this knowledge through their keyboards!

Social tech applications are like any other piece of software implemented in the organization. It takes training to learn them and then apply them productively. When employees are required to figure out how to use them on their own, they will, to some degree. The downside for you is how long it takes them.

In some cases, employees don't use a software application until they get training on it. They don't feel comfortable installing something new and experimenting with it until they figure it out. Because social tech is such a new field, formal training programs haven't been configured for the most part. There's also a sense that these tools can be self-taught.

A look at the historical adoption of new technology shows us that we've been moving in this direction for a while. It would have been unthinkable for someone to be handed a mainframe terminal and told to figure it out. When Microsoft Office tools became widely available, some organizations began to take it for granted that people would know how to use Word, Excel, and PowerPoint, but most provided some type of training if people asked for it. Now we're at a point when many organizations assume that when it comes to Web-based social applications, people will learn on their own.

Self-Training

If we assume that people will invest the time on their own to learn Web-based tools like social tech, we must be aware that this can stunt our growth in applying social tech on the job. If we take a generational view of this, we can generalize some conclusions that indicate we should *not* assume people will self-train.

Observing older generations, we tend to see people less willing to experiment with new technology, and less able to figure out on their own how to use it. Because the younger generations have less anxiety about experimenting with what a software application will do, they tend to learn most of the features faster. They also develop a pattern in their minds as to how social tools should work so moving among applications isn't difficult.

Understanding this dynamic can help you strategize delivery of training, and to whom it should be targeted. Yet, generational profiling isn't 100 percent accurate so you must consider that even some younger people will need training, while a few older people will self-train well.

TRAINING WITH PRACTICAL APPLICATIONS

SMART

MANAGING

One of the quickest ways to get people to leverage training and provide value for the organization is to use live examples that create immediate benefits for the user. For example, if you're going to train people on Twitter, start them out by following ten industry experts who can provide information and resources from Day 1. Don't start them trying to tweet ten times a day when they don't have many followers because they won't see the value for the time invested. People need to see practical results quickly to entice them to use social tools.

There's a continuum of people who at one end never need training, and at the other end never use an application unless trained. It's important for you to realize this and appropriately target your training.

Deep Training, Not Just Signing Up

In April 2010, Citibank surveyed more than 550 small business owners in the United States about social tech use in their organizations, and found that more than 81 percent said they don't use social tech. Yet, most of these will tell you they have signed up for multiple sites. One of the big benefits of training is finding those quick wins so users begin to see how the features may apply. Yet teaching people a few quick examples won't give them the overall knowledge they'll need later. Once you have their attention with a few quick wins, you must go on and teach all the features and options in an application.

In many cases, they won't remember exactly how to do a specific task, but they'll remember that it existed. This makes it easier for them to at least investigate until they discover how to do the task. Deep training gives users the confidence that they really understand all the application can do, even if they haven't mastered every element.

Contrast this with simply teaching people how to sign up for a site, then giving them a quick run-through of the capabilities. Without a few points of value that demonstrate to the user a clear advantage in using the application, you end up with people who understand its basic tenets but never use it. They'll remain "signer uppers."

Who Should Do the Training

Be aware of the dynamics created with *who* delivers the training. As mentioned earlier, there's a lot to like about the concept of reverse mentoring, so having a young person teach a group of older employees about Facebook is sometimes the way to go. This is a great way to let a young staff member gain some pride and impress some of the older teammates. There can even be helpful bonds that get formed between people of different generations who might not otherwise work together closely.

Consider an even better dynamic: have an older person teach their demographic peers! There's an unspoken pressure that gets put into the room when one of the oldest people on the team is clearly able to teach

> **YOUR ONLINE RELEVANCY SCORE—SO WHAT!**
> An example of poor training is teaching people how to do a search on their name or the organization's name, and get a social relevancy score on a site like Socialmention. Once they're made aware of this site, they'll go once, check the scores, and will likely never go back. Go a few steps further and teach them how to have Socialmention e-mail them every mention of their name, and then provide a clear understanding of how each score is calculated. They may then check the site more often because they'll see value to them personally.

everyone how to use a social tool. This also can be a great inspiration for younger people in the room to adopt the tools quickly.

You must also consider doing the training yourself. No other person in front of the room will send the subtle message that you will when you're able to show everyone how to use social tools. Once again, lead by example.

Don't wait to put an organized training program in place. The faster you can get something helpful and consistent in front of your people, the faster you help them learn these tools to reach organizational goals. There's a clear advantage in learning to use these tools before your competition does. The longer you wait, the harder it is to catch up when someone above you in the organization mandates that you get up to speed. Today is the day to either get a training program started or improve the one you've been delivering. Don't assume that because some of your team uses these tools, that everyone is. Nor should you assume that because someone tells you he has signed up for a service that he's getting value from it!

The Responsibility for Researching New Social Tools

New tools are coming out fast, and current tools are going through quick rounds of improvement. Therefore, you need some kind of research process that identifies new tools, and decide whether they should be introduced to the organization. This isn't something that managers have had to take responsibility for yet. It has been the standard operating procedure to let the IT department pick the software standards in the organization, or for people to bring in to the office whatever they use at home.

Social tech creates a new dynamic in how we choose the tools because they are so specific in their use that even among departments and users there might be good reasons to use a variety.

Some people have a natural bias for using the same tools forever. Once they learn them, they have little desire to change. Other people get bored within a few months and look for a better application with more features or a prettier user interface.

The most important aspect of a research process is that you want to make sure the tools you're using are the most productive and feature-rich available. This translates into happier users and more benefits for the organization. In a world where most of the tools and upgrades are free, there's no reason to continue the use of a function-limited tool. However, use some discretion because you can't be changing applications every 30 days.

> **KEY TERM**
>
> **User Interface (UI)** Every piece of software has a look and feel that the user interacts with on the screen. This includes the colors, font, and layout. In some cases, the UI also includes error handling, menu construction, and workflow. Sometimes, users are attracted to a newer and prettier look on the screen even if there's no increased functionality.

You Are the Filter

One of the unintended consequences that can come from researching new sites is the propensity to want to constantly change tools. There has to be a filtering system to make good decisions on when the appropriate time is to upgrade or trade out a tool. In most cases, you are the best filter. This is a difficult decision to make because we all know there will be a better application coming out soon. This doesn't mean you allow people to upgrade to it. There are lots of factors that need to be taken into account. For example:

- What else is going on in the organization and do people have the time to learn a new application?
- Are the new features so beneficial that they offset the investment to learn a new tool?
- Will the new tool be compatible with the other social tools you already use so that you don't have to rebuild the entire contact network of your current application?

- Is the new tool vetted for security?
- Will the new tool cause compatibility problems if part of the team upgrades and the rest do not?

Be careful not to engage in a robust research program without a filtering system. If you do, don't be surprised to see the entire team using different tools to do the same tasks. And don't be shocked when people fail to have the ability to use the tools to connect internally because there isn't consistency across the team.

Manager's Checklist for Chapter 5

☑ New social tools hit the market daily. In some cases, they provide real advances or new capabilities. Although it's impossible to stay current on every new thing, you should at least have some kind of process for staying aware of the big changes.

☑ Although it might be uncomfortable, it's important to adopt new tools when there's clear proof of their worth.

☑ It's important to identify the right tools for the team, and to enforce consistent use where possible.

☑ It's critical for you to use these tools and not just talk about them. Leading by example is always the most powerful form of leadership.

☑ A training paradigm needs to be developed for current and incoming employees, and thought needs to be given as to *who* does the training.

☑ You must ensure that people aren't merely signing up for services but not learning how to use them fully. There's no value in simply signing up.

☑ Assign someone to research and recommend new tools when something more valuable than what you currently use comes out.

☑ You need to play the role of a filter on new tool adoption so that people don't constantly change tools or don't get stuck on an old, unproductive version.

Managing Your Online Reputation

There are three areas of an online reputation that every organization should be concerned about: the entity's reputation, the executives' reputations, and the reputation of your products and services. As we discuss this subject in this chapter, be aware that we are referencing all three.

An online reputation evolves for all three with or without your help. As you can guess, the more you do to assist in the process, the better shot you have at creating a good reputation.

Before we approach what an *online* reputation is, let's review what a standard reputation is considered. The dictionary defines it as:

1. The estimation in which a person or thing is held, especially by the community or the public generally; repute: a man of good reputation.
2. Favorable repute; good name: to ruin one's reputation by misconduct.
3. Favorable and publicly recognized name or standing for merit, achievement, reliability, etc.: to build up a reputation.
4. The estimation or name of being, having, having done, etc., something specified: he has the reputation of being a shrewd businessperson.

In plain language, it means what other people think of you based on a set of data points they have been told about or observed. An online reputation connotes a reputation as described by the collection of information provided on the Web—created both by you, and by the crowd. For all of

> **Online Conversations** Conversations online are made up of
> blogs, tweets, Facebook posts, and comments provided for a
> specific group, and are often interactive in nature. This means
> **KEY TERM**   that opinions, information, and experiences are documented,
> and others have the ability to add their thoughts or respond directly. These
> conversations are stored on servers, potentially for your lifetime, and are
> generally searchable.
>
>   When someone mentions a person, product, or company, that comment
> will be easily found through a number of searches. Tap into a handful of
> conversations about a product, and you will get a quick sense of what peo-
> ple think about it in an unfiltered way. Tap into a mine of personal conversa-
> tions or content postings and you can learn a lot more about a person than
> you might care to know.

history, your reputation was made up of the community of people who
came in contact with you personally, and if you were well-known publicly,
by the press. For the first time in humanity, people and organizations have
a reputation that can be derived from a collection of content, conversations, and comments that are stored electronically. Much of this is out of
our control and that's where the work begins.

A reputation is a powerful influencer of how people treat a person or
an organization, especially if they don't know the individual or organization personally. People generally believe what others say so if three people blog about how you are a jerk, most readers will infer that you're a
jerk. If five people say they love a product, even if one doesn't, people generally believe the product has value. Reputations can make or break a
company, and they can help or hurt your career. They have always been
important to us, and now there is a radical new way that reputations are
being formed and communicated.

To be a strong leader in the use of social tools, you must understand
how a reputation gets formed online, and how you influence how you and
your organization are perceived. Note that when we say "you" we're often
referring to you as an individual and your organization, and the best practices for monitoring and improving them are basically the same. The rest
of the chapter refers to both. We also refer to the process of *online reputation management* (ORM) as the practice of taking a proactive role in influ-
encing how your online relevancy is perceived.

The Three States of a Reputation

There will be one of three clear opinions people will get when they search and find your name mentioned in content, conversations, and posts. This decision on which state your reputation is in gets made quickly in many cases, sometimes simply by glancing at the first page of a Google search! Let's examine these three states of perception:

- **Good.** A good reputation is earned when an observer can easily see that the subject of their search has many connections with people, followers, friends, or contacts. A constant stream of valuable information is published online, and that value is measured in the number of times people resend the information to others. A clearly positive organizational voice that interacts with customers in a human and useful way. Having a positive "sentiment ratio," where many more people say positive things than negative about the brand or the person.

- **Bad.** Just take the reverse of everything said above, and this is how you earn a bad reputation. Have very few connections, publish little content, and what you publish is boring. Don't interact with customers or followers, and have a negative sentiment ratio where people generally say bad things about you and your products.

- **Invisible.** When there is nothing mentioned about you online, and you don't participate on social sites, you'll appear to be invisible. Some people think this is a positive because it's at least not a bad reputation, but the truth is that people assume a negative reputation when you have no relevancy online. Being invisible won't save you.

Whether you choose to play or not, you do have an online reputation that's in one of these three states. The only question is whether you proactively choose to manage yours and the organization's. It really isn't a matter of *if* you'll manage your reputation. It's simply a matter of how and when.

Who Is Forming an Opinion of You Online?

If you had the ability to be notified every time someone searches on your name, you'd be surprised at who looked you up and how many times. It's commonplace for people to search online to learn about products or companies before purchasing, or even before contacting the company to speak to a representative. But it'd be naïve to think that only customers are checking out your online reputation. Investors, partners, vendors, prospective employees, and bankers are a short list of the people outside an organization who are interested in what's published online. On the personal side, prospective employers, friends, business acquaintances, family members, and love interests may bring up your name to see what people are saying.

Only five years ago, searchers online would likely have found a Web site that was built specifically to deliver information about you, or a mention or two on some ancillary Web property. Today, they'll find a plethora of information, including content generated internally. It's published through any one of the many social media/networking sites, and content created by others who mention you. What we say to others either directly or through direct postings provides a body of work about what we are doing at that time, and what we think about the subjects posted. The longer time goes on, the more content each person and organization accumulates. Add to this all the content that others have posted about us, and it makes it easy to see why people are interested in gaining a perspective on a reputation by searching online.

TOOLS

ADDICTOMATIC.COM
Google has become the most common way that people search for the information that makes up a reputation. There are new search tools coming out that give a different glimpse into what people are saying about someone or a brand. Try doing an addic-tomatic.com search and see how they have isolated their search results to a collection of social tech sites. This socially specific search engine shows more directly what people are saying about you or the organization within conversation streams as opposed to static Web pages.

The truth is many people search online to learn about your organization, and they are no longer searching to learn only about your products and services. They are looking to see how other people feel about you, and how much value you create by providing content to the Internet Herd. They can also be pretty harsh critics. When people search online, they're quick to form a negative impression if they see more than one negative comment. When the searchers are potential customers or potential employees, you can see the problem.

Salespeople routinely search on buyers to learn as much personal information about them as they can. Now buyers are searching on salespeople so they can glean how much they really know about the industry, and how long they've been with the company. Prospective employees search on the company, and the company searches on the prospective employees. Small businesses search for information on a bank to work with, and then the lending officer searches for information on the small business. You get the idea. Whatever you can possibly imagine as to the number of people who search for information on you, double it at least!

PERSONAL REPUTATIONS

CAUTION

There's a new Web site that'll be hitting the streets called Honestly.com. This site is specifically built to allow people to comment on each other's feelings about each other. Think of it like a giant public rating system for individuals. They're putting safeguards in place so people can't have all their friends post positive comments—much like Wikipedia uses editors to assure accuracy of information. Even so, some people feel that this site will become a repository for negative comments about people from those they may have wronged over time. This site is a harbinger of things to come in regard to personal online reputations. Whether we like it or not, there'll be information about us online for everyone to see.

The Power of Words

Even though social tech is young, there's already starting to be quite a bit of content online about people and organizations. If you look at the scale of the new content that gets posted daily, you begin to understand that over a few years, there will be many mentions of a name, with both good and bad observations. Add to this the content generated by people and organizations themselves, and you have a potent mix of media, comments, observations, rants, and conversations for all to see. The words now being saved on the millions of servers that make up the Internet are powerful, and out of our control for the most part.

What we say on social sites and what others say about us is the foundation for our online reputations. When customers go online to see how

> **SMART MANAGING**
>
> ## TRAINING PEOPLE ON THE REALITIES OF POSTING CONTENT
>
> There are still people who really don't understand that when they post content or comments they are exposing this to everyone. Just because a person only has 40 people following him or her on Twitter, that does not mean that the tweet he or she sends railing against the current president is unsearchable by everyone else. When it comes to the importance of the words you send over the Internet, people still need to be shown the realities. A smart manager regularly trains his or her people to understand that before they hit the Submit or Send button, they must first be comfortable that whatever they say will be seen by millions (potentially) and stored forever.

other people feel about a product or company, they'll only invest a few seconds in most cases, to get a quick read on how the collective views things. They aren't interested in investing hours to assure they have a "fair" view of a reputation. They'll look at the comments made about whatever they're interested in on a site or two, and usually just on the first page of search results. One negative comment may be enough to send them on their way. Words are powerful.

As we have now seen, employers will search for any information published online about a prospective employee. It only takes one mention of something that can be perceived as a negative, and another candidate may win the job. We form our impressions of people and companies from little actual experience in many cases, and the words that make up an online reputation can be the difference-maker in many cases.

> **CAUTION**
>
> ## TWITTER AND THE LIBRARY OF CONGRESS
>
> The U.S. Library of Congress has asked and been granted the entire database of tweets from Twitter for the first few years. They see the Twitter database as a wonderful glimpse into what was important to citizens at any point in time, and therefore a powerful research tool for historians later. This all sounds great until you realize that every comment you might have made over Twitter will be searchable by anyone in your family tree from now on.

Online Credentials

Another way to view an online reputation is that the body of online content about you or your organization constitutes your online credentials. In many cases people aren't searching to see your reputation per se, they just want to understand how "real" you are. For this reason, it's useful to think of social tech as not only creating an online reputation for you, but also providing a very public set of online credentials.

When viewed in this light, it's easier to understand why we should take a proactive approach in making those credentials as positive as possible. Both organizations and people must invest energy to understand what their online credentials look like to others, and do their best to influence how they are perceived. Online reputations are no longer a spectator sport. We have the ability to improve them, and that takes a plan.

The Three-Step Process for Managing an Online Reputation

I hope at this point you're excited (at least somewhat) about the potential for a good online reputation. The next step is to learn the formula for being able to influence that reputation in the direction you want to see it move.

We've reduced this process to a three-step system that's now being used by the leading organizations to gain measurable results. (1) Listen to what people say about you on the Web. (2) Have a philosophy for engaging people who have commented on you. (3) Have a system for measuring your online relevance.

As we describe the online reputation formula, think about it in terms of the organization and how you might help facilitate each of these steps. Then think about it

> **SMART**
> **INFLUENCING WHAT PEOPLE WILL THINK**
>
> **MANAGING**
>
> It's important to understand that you have some control over your online reputation. This isn't something that just happens to you or that you have no influence over. If you're willing to invest some energy in crafting an online reputation, you'll see positive results. If you sit idly by and pay no attention, people will form their perception based on their searches. A positive online reputation takes an investment of time and energy, but it's worth it.

from your personal standpoint and how you might put lightweight versions of these steps in place to improve your own online presence.

Step One. The Listening Process

First, you must put in place an effective listening process. You do this by using tools that monitor all the social conversations and content uploaded to the social media sites for any mention of the organization, products, and executives' names. These listening tools can be configured to send notices through e-mail, or can gather the mentions into a report. They can send the alerts to you in real time as they find the mentions or gather them up and send a report or e-mail daily or weekly.

LISTENING TOOL OPTIONS
There are a variety of free and subscription-based tools to help you build your listening **TOOLS** process. We suggest using more than one option because you're more likely to find all mentions of a keyword if you stack tools on top of each other. There are subscription-based tools like Viralheat, SM2 (Alterian), and Radian6. Free tools include services like Google Alerts, Alerts.com, Yotify, and Socialmention.com.

Once you have an effective set of listening applications in place, there must be a process for reviewing what's uncovered each day. The faster you respond to negative mentions the better, so it's wise to review mentions as often as possible. For this reason, there should be at least one person assigned to this task as part of his or her job, and there should be a backup who can fill in if that person is gone for more than a day. Obviously if your organization is large, you might have a full-time person who plays this role, or even integrate an online listening system into your normal customer support process to handle the volume.

Once a listening process is put in place, it's a good idea to notify your employees of this fact so they are clear that any mentions of the company name, even in a passing Facebook mention, could show up.

The final to-do in a listening process is to route the mentions you uncover to the people who might benefit from the information. For example, if a competitor is commenting on your products, route this information to the sales and product development teams.

If someone internally is making negative comments about the organization or a customer, route it to the HR department. If a customer is making a negative comment about a product, route this to the cus-

UNANTICIPATED DISCOVERIES

CAUTION

It isn't uncommon that organizations make interesting discoveries when they put a robust listening process in place. Possibilities include employees making negative comments about their work situations or bosses. In some cases, they find employees who are sharing internal information without really understanding how publicly it's being shared.

Before you react out of anger at what you might find, realize that some people don't understand how public their comments are. Look at this as a training moment and use the evidence of their conversations as a tool to teach them a critical lesson about social tech conversations.

tomer's salesperson or the customer support group. Not all online comments are negative so you need to know where to route the positive comments, as well. The routing schema leads us into the second step in the ORM process.

LISTENING FOR COMPETITORS

TRICKS OF THE TRADE

Once you have your listening tools in place, consider turning them toward finding mentions of your competitors and their products. This is a great way to harvest real-time information on what they're doing.

Step Two. An Engagement Policy

Once you've built the capability to harvest mentions of the keywords meaningful to you, a plan for what actions these might trigger must be documented and put in place. We call this an engagement policy because it's a written set of instructions that guide employees on how the organization chooses to respond to the mentions online. There are typical stages organizations go through with social tools and the first is to listen for mentions of their names. Next the listeners lurk on conversations and watch them happen without participating. Then they engage and communicate sparingly to test the waters of using an organizational voice. Finally, they'll interactively communicate in a human way with people who mention them or their products.

The best way to create an engagement policy is to start by documenting all of the types of mentions you might see of negative and positive varieties. For example, your list could look like this:

SMART

MANAGING

TALKING LIKE A HUMAN BEING

When an organization is in the situation of responding to people's comments through social tools, keep in mind they are human beings, and want you to speak to them like you are one as well. That means no carefully crafting responses in corporate speak so that all humor and texture is stripped out. Even when you are speaking on behalf of the organization, use a relaxed and personable tone, especially if you're addressing someone who has written something negative about you. Apologize if you truly have done something wrong. If not, at least acknowledge their opinions before you debate with them. By the way you craft your words you'll either transmit the feeling that you are caring and real, or you'll appear to be a soulless entity.

Positive comments about

- Our products
- Our people
- Our executives
- Something we have done

Negative comments about

- Our products
- Our people
- Our executives
- Actions we have taken
- Our organization in general
- Our customer support

Each of these types of mentions should be forwarded to a specific person or group so they can be dealt with, or at least provide the information to someone who'd benefit from knowing it. Then for each type of mention, agree to a response method. Your options are to not respond at all, to respond through the same medium on which you found the comment, or to find contact information for the person who posted the comment and call him or her directly. You decide how to respond; there's no standard model you must follow.

The goal with this step is to engage people in conversations that enhance positive things they say by sharing them with a wider audience,

GOING OLD SCHOOL WITH A PHONE CALL   SMART

The early engagement policy results that companies are seeing have produced an interesting paradox. The most effective method of turning a negative online comment into a positive customer is to reach out by phone, and not by using an online connection.   MANAGING

People seem to view a quick phone call from a company that they have just posted a negative comment about as a personal and effective way to remedy the situation. Ignoring a comment is the worst thing you can do, and simply responding electronically can be taken as not caring enough. Consider doing a pilot project where your organization calls negative commenters directly and see if you like the results.

gaining the benefit of good public relations. On the other hand, you must learn the skill of turning negative online comments into positive mentions when possible. Many times an engagement policy helps you acknowledge someone with a gripe in a way that results in the person posting a thank you comment because he or she appreciates that you cared enough to address the issue. Both enhancing the positive comments and turning around the negatives can improve your online reputation.

AVOIDING FLAME WARS   TRICKS OF THE TRADE

One critical aspect of an engagement policy is training your people not to create a situation where a heated conversation is publicly inflamed. It's a good policy to interactively engage people who have made negative comments, but at the point that the person posting moves into attacking the organization inappropriately, your people must break off the conversation.

Once you've locked in a solid engagement policy and you're able to see a complete stream of mentions, you can move on to the final step.

Step Three. ORM Measurement and Reporting Systems

As online reputations get more important to our ability to succeed, we must develop ways to measure both where we stand now, and what the trend is showing so that we can see where improvements can be made.

Not only is it important to generate some kind of analysis on where we stand with our online reputations, we need to be able to see what kind of return on our effort we're getting from investing resources to improve things. Of course what you measure has a lot to do with the kinds of information you generate.

Many things can be measured, so the following list isn't meant to be all-inclusive. We're just giving you a place to start:

- Number of mentions (broken down by tweets, blogs, and Facebook mentions)
- The percentage growth of the number of mentions over past months
- Quantity of content posted by the organization (broken down by tweets, blog posts, etc.)
- Number of times organizational posts were passed on to people other than those connected originally (this is a measurement of quality and perceived value of the content)
- The sentiment ratio of positive to negative posts
- The number of negative and positive posts
- Third-party ratings from relevancy measurement sites

As you know, what gets measured gets done. Without a mature and consistent measurement system that shows trends and the results of your efforts, you won't have a way to gauge where you stand or what's helping you make progress. An online reputation is too important to leave to chance or to be in a situation where you are flying blind as to where you stand. For these reasons, we recommend that after you put a great measurement system in place, don't skip repackaging your findings into a report to distribute to others in the organization.

Sharing a dashboard of ORM information with a wide group can be helpful because it calls attention to the subject. It spreads the information about what people are saying and how the organization is perceived. We recommend sending out an e-mail that delivers some of the key measurements and interesting trend metrics once a month. What you'll find is that this raises the importance of this area with the people who have the ability to influence your online reputation.

The elements of a good ORM dashboard report integrate some of the statistics mentioned above with additional samples of both positive and negative mentions, descriptions of responses, and ad hoc stories of successes gained through ORM. It should quickly tell the story of what's going on in the social sphere in case there are employees who don't follow things firsthand. Readers should be able to grasp the important bullet points in just a few seconds so that they don't have to work hard to grasp the key thoughts.

Whatever you do, make sure this report is shared with the executive team. Then they'll be aware of what people are saying out on the streets, and gain some level of buy-in to the concept of an online reputation.

MEASUREMENT SYSTEMS

There are two key mistakes to avoid when measuring an online reputation.

- **Mistake 1:** Running searches on an incomplete list of terms. For instance, running a search on your full name versus your Twitter or Facebook username, or running alerts on the company name, but not the product names.

- **Mistake 2:** Overly reacting to very negative or very positive comments. You almost have to look at this like ice skating judges and throw out the highs and lows and focus on the majority in the middle.

The Tension Between Online Reputation and Privacy

One potentially difficult concept to navigate as a manager is the debate that ensues when people discuss the collision of personal lives with professional careers. For the most part, people have held the belief that these were two separate spheres and the two shouldn't overlap. People should be able to live whatever lifestyle they choose, speak in a vernacular that suits them, and be friends with anyone they like in their personal lives. And further, this should have no impact on their business life.

For some folks this means living two very different lives to the extreme, which means that information leaking from one side to the other would not be a good thing. This has been possible to pull off up until this point. Now, however, people are being forced into a situation where both sides of their lives are becoming part of the overall online reputation picture. For those who don't like this turn of events, the option of online invisibility sounds good.

Even people who are generally OK with exposing their personal lives to people they do business with struggle with this new concept. For generations, people have been taught to be private about the details of their personal lives. This flies in the face of social technologies because online people (in your work world) want to know you, read your thoughts, and freely post information about you. Note this, whether you approve or not, you cannot stop others from making observations about you. We are in the middle of a change in culture from one of privacy, to one of openness and this transition isn't going to be easy.

To build a good online reputation, we must participate, and that means publishing our thoughts and expert opinions so others know what we think and what we're qualified to talk about. We want people to talk about us, and then to pass around the content we publish because they think it's valuable. The reality is we can't at the same time be very private and expect to build a strong online reputation strictly on what others say about us. We have to give up some privacy to show more of ourselves to others. This goes for organizations, as well.

TRICKS OF THE TRADE **GENERATIONAL DIFFERENCES WITH ONLINE REPUTATIONS**
Because young people are growing up with a completely different set of variables of privacy and online reputation, you generally find they're not so worried about privacy. They view putting lots of content about themselves online as a positive because it enhances their ability to quickly filter people who have the same likes and dislikes.

The older generations often view having lots of online information published about them as an imposition on their privacy. They're sensitive to the separation of personal and professional information and their personal opinions about life versus thoughts about their vocation. A savvy manager proactively works to help reign in the younger generations from oversharing online and urges the older generations to be willing to share more of themselves where appropriate.

Hiring and Employee Research

The issue of privacy versus an online reputation comes into focus when a person applies for a job with your organization. Nearly all applicants have some kind of background screening done on them. In many cases this includes running a number of online searches to see what's there and what others have said about an applicant.

In the old days, a person went to an interview, provided a few references, and the decision would get made on hiring them or not. It's a different world now. Back in those same old days it was difficult to really learn much about a person from the interview process. Now it's incredible what can be learned about a person with five minutes of searching, and some percentage of what you will find will be personal in nature. This ability to get this level of insight into someone is powerful, and we need to really consider how to handle it well.

There's been a ton of articles written that detail the stories of people who have failed to get a job or lost a job because of something they have posted online. There are also situations where someone's online reputation has taken a serious hit because of something posted by a friend. This dynamic is only going to continue as we see people flocking to join social sites and using them to communicate with their contacts. Those who are searching for information need to take into account that we all have both personal and professional lives. We all make mistakes, and many people might behave differently in more informal personal settings than they do on the job. This doesn't mean improper personal behavior should be overlooked, but at least recognize the timing of events, and conditions under which comments were made.

Another new phenomenon impacting reputations is the *cross group infection* that happens when a person comments on a different group's site, and creates a flow of information that becomes embarrassing. For example, a mother friends her daughter on Facebook. The daughter posts on her wall a comment about a boy she thinks is cute. The mother jumps in and posts an admonition that her daughter should look elsewhere.

THE JILTED GIRLFRIEND

One unlucky job applicant found out the hard way that an ex-girlfriend with deep social tool skills can cause havoc. After he broke up with her (nicely and for good reason), she went on an organized campaign to smear his name in the social space. She tweeted about him, posted many Facebook comments, and wrote entire blogs about their travails.

With no particular way to defend himself without escalating the situation, he was forced to explain the situation every time he was interviewed. His track record as an employee and student was stellar, yet each person who visited with him sooner or later got around to asking him who this woman was. In this case, he was guilty of nothing more than making a poor choice in girlfriends.

KEY TERM

Cross Group Infection One of the new dynamics created by participation in eCommunities like Facebook, Foursquare, and MySpace is the dreaded problem of mixing groups we belong to. The reason this can be a problem is that what we choose to share with one group we may not want shared with the others. For example, when one group is your family, another your friends, and then your office mates, you have three constituencies that might all speak a different vernacular and have different relationships with you. Cross group infection comes in when you share information with one group that somehow bleeds over into the other group. The classic example is one of your friends uploading an inappropriate (but funny) picture of you from your vacation together in Las Vegas that your boss finds.

Then the daughter's friends post a tirade of comments filled with expletives about the boy. These show up on the mother's wall now since she had joined the conversation. If you saw this in a search of the mother's page, what would you think of her?

Let's look at a couple other real-world examples you may run into if you haven't already. You have a stack of résumés sitting in front of you and decide you're going to run a quick addictomatic.com search to see what you might find on the people who are coming in today for interviews.

The first candidate is 24 years old and a heavy Facebook user. A quick glance of his site reveals a couple of negative comments about his current employer and a picture from a bachelor party that shows he and his friends clearly having a good time at a lake party. It also details the fact that he recently broke up with his girlfriend and it was not a happy experience from his viewpoint, based on the harsh comments he has and his memory of her. None of these things is particularly horrible, but they do paint a picture of someone who might have some issues you would be happy to avoid.

The second candidate is 36 years old and with an unusual last name. This is important because it makes it simple to run a search and find information about him. Yet you are surprised to find virtually no information on the Web. He has a LinkedIn profile that hasn't been touched in a year and has few connections. Other than that, he evidently doesn't participate online at all, and no one seems to be interested in talking about him.

How do you integrate what you have found online into your decision? Should you look at the first candidate through a negative filter because of what you observed about his personal life? And is the second candidate actually preferable because he's invisible? Or, do you take this as a sign that he has a lot to hide, or simply has not progressed in learning how to use social tech as a tool? My point here is that managers must be careful about how they use the power of access to online reputations. The opinions you glean from what you find could lead you in a wrong direction on a hiring decision if you're not careful.

Online Relevancy Scores

One last important concept to understand about online reputations is the fact that we're close to a time where we'll all be universally scored with a "social relevancy" measurement. This means individuals and organizations. There are already Web sites that are refining algorithms that take into account the amount of content published, the percentage of time that content is forwarded to others, the number of connections, and the sentiment ratio, to give a person or organization a social relevancy score. Much like a credit score, you may not know exactly how it was calculated, but whether you want it or not, one will be calculated on you for anyone who wants to grab that information.

This score can be calculated by combining a collection of your usernames across social applications, or if you are an organization, by doing searches on the entity and product names. Even today you can go to sites like socialmention.com and klout.com and see scores on how much social influence you have on the Web. You can imagine how this will impact recruiting and marketing at the point that the general public begins to trust these scores as accurate representations of a person's or brand's relevancy in the world.

If you think about what this chapter is about, you may recognize that for the first time in human history, it'll be possible to learn a lot about an entity in an instant. Not just famous people or well-known organizations, but regular people who've been anonymous, for the most part, in the past. Not only will you be able to see information they publish about themselves, you'll also be able to tap into comments others have made about them. Instead of being forced to learn by experience what a person or organization is like, you can now find out in an instant what the crowd thinks of them.

This will be a more dramatic change for humanity than most people realize.

Manager's Checklist for Chapter 6

☑ Online reputations are going to become critical to career advancement—especially for you personally. It's common for someone to search your name to see what information is available.

☑ You need to be able to evaluate fairly what you find online about recruits or current employees. This means taking multiple factors into account before you make judgments on what you see or don't see online.

☑ The line between personal and professional is getting thinner online. It's going to be a tough decision between what's private versus building a robust online presence.

☑ You must understand how to respond to good and bad comments made online about you personally and the organization. You must also teach those around you this same skill.

☑ You must play a central role in helping the organization develop an online reputation process: listen, engage, measure.

☑ Managers must manage their personal online reputations to protect their careers and provide a good model for their people.

Building Rivers
of Information

There's a new Web dynamic created by the advent of social tools that can only be described as an explosion in the channels that provide information, opinions, thoughts, media, infographics, and statistics.

These channels are made up of information distribution systems like blogs, eNewsletters, twitter streams, RSS feeds, Facebook posts, discussion streams, and Web alerts. This doesn't count systems that were built to push topic-specific types of information to people. The result of our world having access to these tools is that literally billions of people can now send information to billions of others. No filters from media companies, no costs to pay, and no way to stop where it might go and who might read it.

The analogy we like to use is that all this adds up to a raging "river of information." We used to have a small trickle of information that we fed to our minds each day, now we have the potential of dumping in a torrent of information. This is scary for some, overwhelming for others, and a serious career advantage for those who learn to leverage this new concept.

Along with these ever-growing channels of content distribution, we have an exploding number of people and organizations feeding these systems. The ultimate outcome is a massive flow of information that's now available at our fingertips, if we know how to harness it.

The scale of the volume of information now flowing around the Internet each day isn't something that most people understand. Here's a simple analogy: understand that if you took all the books ever written, you wouldn't equal the amount of content that gets created and sent around the world each week over the Internet. Most of what's getting created is classified as UGC (user-generated content). On top of all the UGC, there's professionally developed content that organizations put out either for marketing or to inform the public on a specific topic.

COMPETITIOUS.COM

FOR EXAMPLE A great example of an information provider. It provides a service that pushes information about competitors that you're interested in tracking. It uses e-mail as the delivery vehicle to update you about changes in competitors' Web sites, press releases that go public, and other interesting bits of information. This could be considered one small tributary in your overall river of information.

User-Generated Content

KEY TERM One of the new abilities that sites like YouTube, Scribd, SlideShare, and Flickr have created is an ability to create your own content (media) and upload it so everyone else on the Internet can view it. The result of this is that sites like YouTube say that the public uploads more than 20 hours of video every minute. You can imagine that this dramatically dwarfs the amount of content created by professional producers.

This river of information is a gift. Humanity up to this point has only had access to a trickle of information because it was filtered by geography, language, press, governments, or cost. Whereas today, we're blessed to live in a time when the information flow is now vast, unfiltered, and easily searchable. The trouble is, many people don't understand how to leverage the gift we've been given.

Rivers of the Past

We've always created creeks of information that could help us be smarter, what we call raising our career IQ. Some people are more likely to invest time studying this material than others. There's a natural difference in people's drive to learn. Decades before the Internet was invented, there were a few people who created powerful rivers of information, but in their case they did this by consuming reams of paper documents a day.

The channels of information we had in the past were newspapers, magazines, industry periodicals, TV, radio, and books. Although these tributaries to a river had plenty of infor-

> **Career IQ** Refers to the level of intelligence you have about the information that's critical to your specific career path and industry. This includes historical knowledge and, more importantly, knowledge of timely information that could be useful in your position.
>
> **KEY TERM**

mation, it was generally pretty stale by the time we received it. A narrow supply group also provided this content, in most cases just six to eight sources, and many of those were getting the information from each other. For some people, this is still an accurate description of where they get most of their knowledge.

The sad thing for people who still rely on traditional media for all their information is that the Web and social tools provide a whole new paradigm for how we can gather, sort, and filter information. This allows us now to create vast rivers of information that dwarf traditional media in scope and quality. The outcome of assembling a powerful Internet-based river of information is that it can provide a volume of knowledge that can make a difference in how people perform on the job. All we need do is make a conscious effort to harvest all the most relevant streams of information.

The impact of improving your river of information cannot be overstated. We stand on the precipice of adding a new skill that can have a dramatic impact on your ability to be effective. Since most of the information of assistance to you is free, there's no cost barrier. The only investment you or your people need to make is the time it takes to identify the information in this river, implement the software tools to help you gather and filter it, and then devote the ongoing time to review what floats by your eyes and ears.

Why Rivers of Information Are Critical

A common saying these days is "Knowledge is power." And the more you know, the better decisions you can make. The better decisions you make, the more successful you will be at whatever you are tasked with doing. Lack of information punches holes in your knowledge base and when a competitor has more knowledge than your organization has, there's a risk that they'll make the moves that reap the rewards instead of you. Most people under-appreciate the raw power of information, and getting it quicker than others. They believe whatever data flow they have now must be OK because they're doing OK. If you want to be *more* than just OK, this is a free and easy skill to learn.

It's impossible to verify this figure, but to put a picture in your mind, it's likely true that each one of us becomes aware of only 5 percent of the information about our profession that we really could leverage. Yet we probably believe we know much more. Only at some point in the future when we actually have the ability to filter and capture a higher percentage will we realize how crude our learning process is today.

WHAT YOU DON'T KNOW CAN HURT YOU

CAUTION When first approaching people to help them implement their social rivers of information, you might run into team members who can't imagine there's any information out in the Websphere that could help them, or that they already get everything they need from offline methods. These are what we call "unconscious incompetents"—they don't know what they don't know. You must gain the skill of showing these people the value of integrating online streams of information into their overall rivers so they'll open their minds to the concept. Fail to do this, and you won't even be able to get them to step one.

More Information Is Better

Two conditions have created our ability to harness powerful rivers. The first is the staggering volume of information now available. When you have 1.8 billion people with the tools to provide information, content, and opinions, and forward materials to the rest of the world, you can imagine that changes the volume of the flow. Add to that the millions of organizations that are coming to depend on the Web as a source of cheap content delivery, and you have what we see today, and that's a mind-bending flurry of information flying around the Internet.

Some of this information is archived and will be important from now on. Other pieces of information may be contained in conversations that will be stored for a while, and then will go away as companies purge their databases. One thing we should all remember is we're still in the early days of these tools, so if we have a flurry of information now, we'll have a complete white-out in a few years. Knowing this, gaining the skills of aggregating and filtering large volumes of information so it can be personally digested will be critical. Failure to learn how to do this means you'll be left on the sidelines of the knowledge economy!

With all due respect to Malcolm Gladwell and his book *Blink*, in which he statistically shows that many decisions can be made accurately by instinct and small amounts of data, most people would rather have access to the full set of facts. Even if a decision can be made correctly 85 percent of the time with just a small amount of data, there are some decisions that really need to be more like 100 percent accurate. The last 15 percent accuracy in making the decision will come from having better access to more information. If you don't believe this, would you go to a surgeon who only knows enough to be accurate with 85 percent of your surgery? Would you want a lawyer who only knows 85 percent of the facts in your case? How about a CPA who only knows 85 percent of the tax law on your return?

Real-Time Information and Reacting Quickly

The second condition driving the massive flow of information is the speed at which we're receiving it. One of the hot areas in technology today is the concept of "real time." This means that information is delivered in seconds from the time the event happened. A good example of this is the fact that Twitter now has become an almost real-time source of news. Within moments of any event, a citizen journalist nearby will be tweeting, taking pictures, and uploading them over Twitter, and possibly even recording video and uploading it, as well. This essentially creates a real-time news source.

There are many situations in the business world where

> **Citizen Journalism** A regular person who isn't a paid professional writer who publishes his or her **KEY TERM** thoughts about an event. It's the power of people to provide news and opinions directly to each other without involving traditional media sources. Not only will they provide text, they can also provide pictures and video right from the site of the event. For this we can thank an explosion in the number of people carrying cell phones with built-in cameras.

having *earlier* access to information allows a person to take advantage of a changing situation faster than the competition. For example, the news that a powerful salesperson has resigned from a competitor might be leveraged if you can offer a job before anyone else. Or the news that a competitor has fallen on hard times could trigger moves toward an acquisition, or to take away customers while the company is distracted.

Clearly, the company that gets this news first is in the best position to take advantage of it. For many reasons, the pace of business, and the world in general, is speeding up. Real-time access to information gives you an edge that might be needed to survive, much less win. When an organization supports a collective ability for every employee to tap into the river of information, no opportunity slips by.

OK, now that you have a picture of what the river is and why it's important, let's put a process in place that siphons off meaningful information to raise your career IQ and then integrating this process into your day.

How to Build a Powerful River of Information

There are a few challenges you might run into when designing and monitoring your river. Although the concept may sound simple, the volume, speed, and never-ceasing flow of what comes across the Internet can make building an efficient river of information tough. Over the coming decade this will become an important career skill that will get refined as people learn and share best practices. We're being handed free online tools to help in constructing and using your river. This is making the job simpler all the time.

We have some early tools to work with, and the process for building a river has already been defined by some early pioneers. These people have reduced this to an art form where a person can gain access to the most important pieces of information critical to their lives with the least amount of time invested. From them we've developed a simple set of steps that you can follow to build yours. Pay attention and be sure to invest enough time and energy in each to implement them. The price for being sloppy in any step is missed information that could be critical to your success!

The great thing about adding this capability to your inventory of skills is that the construction process can be done in a day. From that point forward, the investment is monitoring, saving, and passing on the bits of information that can be helpful to you or the organization. The other task is to constantly improve your sources of information and the tools you use to aggregate and filter them. As with many skills that require up-front training then demand ongoing improvement, building a river of

INVEST THE TIME UPFRONT

The simple three-step process we are about to show you can easily be taught to others. Be warned, however, that if a person doesn't invest the time to fully implement any one of the steps, it will negatively impact the results. This is especially true of the early steps in setting up the process. For example, if you fail to identify the most useful sources of information, much of the daily work to monitor it will go to waste.

information is easy to start, then takes the rest of your life to refine.

Step One. Identify the Sources

First you must select your personal river from the overall ocean. For most people, we're only interested in a tiny fraction of the overall categories of information that are streaming around the world. To the extent that we can define what information is beneficial to us and then find the best sources, we've discovered a powerful flow of information we can act on. Most people have little idea how much information is available in their field. Truth be told, many people would tell you they have 80 percent visibility into the information they need, when the reality is they have 5 percent at their fingertips.

To locate valuable sources of information for your river, you have a couple of options. The first is to interview lots of people around you and find out what they're using to gain information. This provides a great start. The second step is to search online for sources you haven't found to this point. This can be done by using tools like blogged.com to search through their index of bloggers to find ones in your field, or twellow.com, which provides the same service for Twitter users. Industry associations put out many sources of digital information these days. Industry analysts provide reports, some free, and others for a fee. Depending on the field you're in, the government provides information that could be helpful.

Running alerts on keywords can yield new sources of information, as

TRICKS OF THE TRADE

KEYWORD ALERTS

Using alerts on specific keywords from your industry is a simple task. There are numerous free services such as Google Alerts, Yotify, Socialmention alerts, and Alerts.com that will let you track any mention of a keyword from your industry, and send you an e-mail with the link where you can find the information. Run a sophisticated set of alerts for three months and you'll discover hidden streams of information that others may never find.

you can discover people commenting on your field that you wouldn't have found otherwise.

You only need to invest a few hours asking people around you what electronic sources of information they're using and another few hours of intelligent searching, to build a strong initial source of information. Once you tap into a new list of information sources, you'll see immediate results. This step is critical because the steps that follow won't matter much if you don't have a powerful and relevant wellspring of information coming in.

Step Two. Choose Your Tools

Once you've tapped into a strong flow of information, you'll need tools to help you aggregate, filter, store, and pass on this information. The good news about this is many entrepreneurs have identified these needs as well, so we have new tools being provided constantly to help us do each of these tasks. Let's take each area individually and look at how to do it, and what tools can be helpful.

- Aggregating the information flow means using applications to consolidate many sources of information onto one screen. This is important because it takes too much time to scan your river for the important things if you have to go to 50 places to even find the information. It's possible to actually have most of your information literally come to one screen using tools like Google Reader and NetVibes. There are also tools like Tweetdeck and HootSuite that we described earlier.

- Filtering information is the process of routing or highlighting bits of information that have a much higher chance of being important than others. This is where tools like the alert systems come in. Add to alerts tools like competitious.com, mentioned earlier, and you have the ability to highlight pieces of information that are the most important.

Even within tools like Google Reader, you can do searches of your information streams to pull out keywords so you can more quickly see specific pieces of meaningful information. You can even set it up so content from your more useful sources is sent to your e-mail so you never miss seeing it.

- Storing information means having a way to archive information you run across that might be needed later. Generally, the flow of information is so large, even when you take your small percentage, trying to go back and find something you saw two months ago is a challenge. For this reason, it's helpful to have storage processes for anything you believe might be needed in the future.

Do this by creating documents, presentations, and spreadsheets where you add pieces of information as you go along so that you've indexed documents by subject, which makes it easy to find something later. There are also tools like Evernote and Onenote that help users quickly archive pieces of information.

- Having ways to forward information is critical because as you see bits of information that you know would be helpful to others, you need "one click" abilities to route information to a person or a group. This helps you give back to the river by being a type of filter yourself. The people around you will place a high value on being connected with you because they'll see you have a good eye for useful information. Some people will want to use e-mail as a delivery source to redistribute interesting things they find. Others will want to create personal blogs,

PERSONAL PREFERENCES **SMART**

You'll find a wide variability in people's comfort with how they build their rivers, and what tools they choose. **MANAGING**

Don't push them to do things in a specific way. It's more important they find a way to gain the information that's comfortable for them than to be standardized. Some people will want to store information in Word docs, and others will want to use online archives. Some people will want to aggregate news feeds with an e-mail-based RSS reader and others with Google Reader.

or use tools like Tweetdeck and TBUZZ to forward information to groups. Expose your people to the possibilities in this area, but don't force them to use a specific tool they won't be comfortable with.

■ There's not a single way to do any of these steps or a set of tools that's perfect for everyone. Managing information flow becomes a very personal thing that depends a lot on the volume you want to handle and your comfort level with Web-based versus offline tools. As you help your employees leverage powerful rivers, don't feel that you have to dictate exactly how they do it. You'll have more success teaching them the value of the process and holding them accountable for monitoring it in some way every day.

Step Three. Develop a Process for Working Your River Each Day

Once you have great sources of information and the tools to collect them, you need to actively discover, digest, and pass on the important pieces of information you find each day. Note that we said "each" day. With the volume of information you have going through your river, it's not wise to miss working it for a few days. The result of this is that you'll have to do such a cursory review of everything you have siphoned off of the big river that you're likely to miss important pieces.

The No. 1 comment people give when exposed to this concept is, "I don't have time to fit this in my day. I'm already swamped." There's no sense debating whether people really have time in their day or not, because most people feel like they're already full up. Everyone must

SMART

MANAGING

THE RETURN ON INVESTMENT

If you run into a situation where people roll their eyes and tell you they don't have time to create, much less review, a river of information, you might consider giving them this feedback: One of the reasons we're all so busy is that we've accumulated tasks that we believe are important and over time we've continued to do each one of them without reevaluating what might be dropped. People who don't believe they have time to implement a river of information in their careers often are investing time in things that don't provide a return on investment. Help them review what they're spending their time on to see if they can find 30 to 45 minutes that could be spent raising their career IQ.

choose what they find most valuable to invest their time in and learning to leverage a powerful river of information is clearly something that can help your employees and the organization in many ways.

There's no perfect way to integrate the river of information process into your day. Each of us operates differently and ingests information uniquely. Some people need to sit down and review their entire river all in one setting. Others can do it five minutes at a time throughout the day. Generally, it should take no more than 30 to 45 minutes to scan through a normal volume each day. You should look for the information that will be most germane to what you do. It doesn't make sense to try and read every word that you receive. You have to think of it like doing triage. You want to scan through the documents and headlines and look for things that really intrigue you and focus on those.

Here's a list of possible options to consider when creating your specific method of reviewing your river:

- Reviewing the river once a day, preferably in the morning, helps get through it so it doesn't become a distraction during the day. Triage videos or Web sites you might want to view later by saving them in browser tabs and review them when you have free time in between things.

- Split up content as to where it's directed. Send text-based content to your laptop and videos to your mobile device, for instance. This way you have content on multiple devices so you have things to review regardless of your travel or location situation.

- Rank the importance of content in your river and send the critical items to your e-mail so you're sure to review them each day as you do e-mail. Send the less important streams to other applications to be reviewed when you have the time to devote to it.

- Be sure to mix media and delivery types so you're getting information in newsletters, blogs, tweets, video, audio, etc. This helps keep your interest, and assures a dynamic spread of content and ideas.

- Always be on the lookout for new aggregation and filtering tools to help you better handle the flow of information. Don't get stuck on one way of handling your river to the exclusion of new ones. Tools come out every week, so look out for new ways of handling things.

> **TWITTER UN-FOLLOWING**
>
> **FOR EXAMPLE**
>
> Twitter provides a great example of a place where you need to constantly be editing whom you follow. You might find ten people in your industry to follow today, and by the end of the month, it's become clear that five of them tweet entirely too much of the time about their personal lives. If this happens, drop them and find more valuable content sources. Don't follow people who just clutter your river with waste.

There's one important thing you must do while reviewing content, and that is constantly evaluate the importance of a specific feed. Don't start off with 30 good sources, then look up a year from now and you're still reviewing the same list. Always be on the lookout for new sources, and be willing to terminate information from a source that's become weak over time. Your river is a living source of information and must be pruned and added to each time you see something better. Fail to do this and you'll find you're investing precious time in something that's become stale.

Helping Your Employees Build Their Rivers

Once you feel comfortable with the process, share this skill with the people around you. Creating a river of information that's deep and valuable allows people to get up to speed on an industry or profession in just a matter of months. If you can teach them to quickly ingest the content each day and continuously refine their information sources, you'll have taught them a skill that will benefit them throughout their careers.

There's a multiplying dynamic that happens when a team of people can build and use rivers of information. This happens because the team will pass on critical pieces of information to each other so that everyone benefits. The team shares sources of information because they know everyone is trying to build a powerful river. The result is a team that has all the information it needs to make great decisions.

Documenting the Baseline Sources

One thing you can do to aid new team members is to document a baseline set of sources that everyone should be reviewing. You then have a list of sources of you can provide to new people, giving them a stream they can immediately tap into. From this starting point, the person can add a handful of new sources based on his or her specific position and needs.

> ### THE STARTER LIST
>
> **FOR EXAMPLE**
>
> A good starter list of sources includes approximately 25 to 30 sources. These should be a mixture of eNewsletters, blogs, twitterers, video blogs, podcasts, and alerts (on competitors or product types). The list should have short descriptions of why someone should follow each source and what he or she can expect from reviewing the information.

This should be a living document that's updated every quarter so the sources are kept fresh and valuable. A quick way to create this document in the beginning is to gather your team and have everyone write down his or her top ten sources of electronic information today. You can aggregate this list into the top 25 or 30 sources for the entire team, as well as the new team members.

Rivers and Accountability

An important step for you is to define some kind of accountability process to assure that people are using these rivers, and continually updating them with new sources of information. If you don't inspect what you expect, you may find that people get sloppy with this discipline. Accountability can range from periodically checking in with people to see that they're reviewing their river, to having them report on something interesting they've found each week.

> ### RIVER REPORTING
>
> **TRICKS OF THE TRADE**
>
> One technique with multiple benefits is to require each team member to report to the others regularly with something they've seen in their river that was interesting. Set up an expectation that everyone does his or her best to provide the most interesting bit of information. Give out periodic rewards or compliments to the people who have uncovered the most intriguing piece of news or idea.

You may find that people will be diligent in the early days of setting up a river, and then get sloppy and stop monitoring it. This can lead to checking it out once a week, then once a month, then almost never. This happens because people make an unconscious decision that working their river is not important enough to invest the time. If this happens, either their information sources are weak, or they simply didn't give the process enough of a chance to experience its true value.

You'll find that if you hold people accountable to give it a fair shot for a month or so, they'll learn the value and will be fine integrating it into their day from that point forward.

Institutionalizing the River

Building personal rivers of information is a good example of a social technology concept that needs to be shared with the whole organization. If you're involved in human resources you could create a list of information sources that can be reviewed by anyone who comes on staff. This can be handed out with the rest of the employment documents. You rarely hear of anyone teaching people how to leverage the Internet in this way. Yet helping people get up to speed quickly on your industry and the news in it can give the overall team a decided advantage. Even an hour of training on the information sources could pay off handsomely.

We mentioned earlier the powerful dynamic that happens when a small team begins to share information. The same holds true across an organization. When everyone invests in creating and working rivers of information, they can share critical pieces of information. Not only will the individual career IQs go up, the overall institutional IQ will rise. And since knowledge begets power, a more knowledgeable organization translates into a more powerful entity.

As a leader, building your own personal river of information is a good example for others. Each time you forward some interesting bit of content, you're telling others how important you think this capability is. You'll know you've achieved success when you start to look forward to reviewing your river each day. We hope you get to the point where you *know* this practice is giving you a market advantage. Do this well, and one day you'll realize that you know something about most subjects that come up in your field because you've seen it discussed in your river. Pass this skill on to your people, and you'll raise the collective IQ in ways that will truly make a difference for the organization.

Manager's Checklist for Chapter 7

☑ Rivers of information are a powerful source of continuing education that cost nothing but a little time.

☑ You must take responsibility for teaching employees how to leverage this, and hold them accountable if you want results.

☑ Create a written list of the baseline sources of information that are best for your market and provide them to the team and new employees.

☑ Follow the three steps to leverage the river. First, discover all the sources of information feeds that can help you. Then, assemble the software tools that will help aggregate, filter, store, and pass on the interesting bits. Finally, review the river for 30 to 35 minutes each day.

☑ Most people will tell you they like the concept but don't see how they can fit it in their day. This usually means they do not see the return on their investment. Knowledge is valuable and well worth the investment if people will give it a try.

☑ Assure that people are always updating the river with new sources, and they play a positive role by passing on new sources to others.

☑ Lead by example and build a powerful river that puts you on top of the latest information, and then pass on the information to others.

Managing the Organizational Voice

S ocial tools provide new options for organizations to "talk" to their constituents. These communication channels can be real time, full of links to additional resources, valuable for the constituents, and free. They give an organization the ability to speak as if it were a person, with a personality that reflects what the entity is about. We call this the "organizational voice." The tools used to deliver the organizational voice are systems like e-mail, Twitter, blogs, Facebook, RSS feeds, and the social media sites like YouTube, Scribd, SlideShare, and Flickr. Whether a message is delivered through an information stream or through a piece of media, it's the organization talking to people in a unique voice.

This capability helps firms create new levels of relationships and changes the ways many sell their products and services. Behind this organizational voice are the human beings who represent it, and this makes managing the process of supporting that voice critical. The voice must be accurate, human-sounding, of use, and interesting. *Ensuring that the many people who actually make up the voice stay on the same page is now your job.*

We're quickly finding uses for this new capability. Organizations now have to decide whether to have an employee communicate under his or her own banner, versus representing the institution as a whole. Let's review a few examples of when organizations may choose to use the cen-

AT&T CUSTOMER SERVICE When AT&T customer service people text message customers to follow up on service calls, they often sign the message as coming from AT&T. Not Bob at AT&T. This little detail and the language he uses humanizes the company by making the communication sound as if it's from a friend, instead of a large company.

tral voice instead of using an employee's:

- When providing answers to support questions delivered over the Web
- When delivering ongoing conversations with Twitter or Facebook to build a connection base, provide value to customers, and deliver marketing information

- When providing corporate communications and investor information to the general public over the Web
- When making product or service announcements
- When replying to blogs
- When engaging with people who comment on the company in any social tech site
- When making product announcements

Having an organizational voice isn't new in that institutions have used advertising and press releases for years to talk to people. Advertis-

WHOLE FOODS TWITTER STREAM A great example of a company speaking with an organizational voice is the twitter stream provided by the Whole Foods Grocery store. They talk to nearly two million customers daily through this channel. Check it out and notice the recipe of content provided in this conversation.

ing is also a strictly one-way form of communicating, and is limited to the company promoting a product or service. It's essentially the organization shouting at people to get their attention. Oh, and it's expensive in most cases. When Web sites and e-mail came along, some organizations tried to use these mediums to be more interactive with people. To the extent that an organization tried to use e-mail too frequently, it was viewed as spamming, especially if the conversation was a sales pitch. E-mail newsletters were the best option we had to deliver an organizational voice, but even these were more like magazines delivered electronically than something that resembled a conversation.

We've recently been handed a whole new toolbox of channels for communicating. Tools like Facebook, blogs, and Twitter provide new options for channels that people can choose to connect with to have an ongoing conversation. Blogs typically have a page or two of conversation, while Twitter (microblogging) only provides 140 characters in which to deliver a message. In many cases, tweets are nothing more than headlines to a link that's attached so a person can connect to a larger piece of information. In both cases, the reader has the ability to comment on or join the conversation.

These new tools are a different animal than what we've had in the past. They let people voluntarily subscribe to a conversation/information feed. The feeds are free to deliver, regardless of the number of followers/readers. They enable readers to comment on the content provided, and then to communicate with each other. The content can be delivered as text, audio, video, or graphics. It can be forwarded to thousands of people in someone's network with a couple of keystrokes. In many cases, these conversations are archived and searchable for years.

Yes, it is a *very* different world now with information delivered through a socially augmented organizational voice!

There is value for an organization in creating multiple channels that communicate to the crowd. This allows the operation to reinforce the brand elements it strives for by creating a tone and feel in the voice it uses to deliver content. If you want to be viewed as a company with a sense of humor and one that is clever and progressive, you can show this in how you talk to people.

There's no other form of advertising that can reach as many people for

---

KNOW WHEN YOU'RE SPEAKING FOR THE ORGANIZATION **SMART**

One of the difficult things for people to understand is that how you identify yourself has everything to do with who the reader perceives is talking to them. For example, if you state your name and title in a response, it's clear you're representing the organiza- **MANAGING** tion. If you reply to a comment that someone else has made to one of your organizational social assets (e.g., the company twitter or Facebook feed) it's perceived as a response on behalf of the organization in general.

WITH THE TOUCH OF A KEYSTROKE Companies like JetBlue and Zappos Shoes have nearly two million followers on Twitter as of this writing and the growth rate doesn't appear to be slowing. In each case there are a handful of people who have permission to post content. Imagine the embarrassment if one of them posts something that's misspelled, or contains incorrect grammar. Even worse, what if someone posted something that was later proven to be untrue? There is no way to unclick the Submit button once something has been posted.

such a small cost or provide an interactive ability to communicate. If you handle the conversation well (as we describe shortly), you can *earn the right* to market your products every once in a while and people will respond positively (in some cases by clicking on a link and buying something).

There are also dangers in letting employees use social tools to speak for the organization by putting words into the company's mouth (so to speak).

Who Listens to These Voices?

So big deal, organizations now have new ways to talk to people. Who actually listens, and what's more, who cares? That's a good question! It turns out that millions of people are listening and they're finding lots of value. In fact, there's a spiral created when an organization builds followers through social communications.

The more people who follow an organization, the more effort the organization puts into providing a valuable stream of information. The more valuable that stream, the more people tell others about it and the more people join the conversation. This is why we're seeing some of these conversations (information streams) blossom to huge numbers of followers in a short time.

There are other specific reasons people sign up to hear an organizational voice, and smart managers are quickly coming to understand these drivers:

- Access to discounts or coupons that only get delivered through this channel. Once word gets out that there are great discounts provided as part of the conversation, the word of mouth kicks in and people race to be part of the information stream.

- People love to hear what others say about a brand they're using, and to communicate with others who like the same companies. For example, followers of a company find lots of value in seeing the comments made by other customers they never would hear otherwise.
- People are motivated to follow any conversation from an organization that gives them earlier access to information than they would get through traditional channels.
- Once people discover that inside information about products might be delivered through this channel, they'll sign up so they can be the first to know.

> ### H&M STORES
> H&M is an international retail giant that has more than one million friends on Facebook. Their customers are fans who love to chat with each other and visit with the company through this channel. The H&M page is like a giant discussion group that could never have happened before the advent of social tools.
>
> **FOR EXAMPLE**

- Some people simply love and support organizations and appreciate being kept updated daily on the happenings.

Many of these organizational conversation streams provide helpful information about the use of their products. This includes everything from recipes on the Whole Foods Twitter stream to travel hints on the Jet-Blue Twitter stream.

Entities that use blogs as an organizational voice often provide the latest information through this channel first, so if you have a need to stay up to the minute on their doings, this may be the best way to do so.

The bottom line is that the list of people who will connect to an organization in this way is growing. In addition, people are getting more comfortable sharing valuable resources with each other so once a stream of information is created and identified, the eWord of mouth dynamic kicks in, and many more will connect and listen.

Managing Employee Participation

There are a number of best practices that would be better learned from this book than by making public communication mistakes. As mentioned previously, behind every organizational voice there are people (or a person) who represents the entity. These people have a critical responsibility because they must not only provide content that will be valuable to readers, they often are called on to drive revenue, as well. Around both of these goals is the need to use a vocabulary and style that represent the tone and feel the organization wants to provide to the readers.

SOUTHWEST AIRLINES HAS ITS BEST DAY EVER

FOR EXAMPLE Southwest Airlines was one of the first airlines to move to an online reservation system, and has heavily leveraged this capability to keep costs down. In the last year the company has twice run discounts through Twitter as the single delivery source, and on each day this was done Southwest set records for online sales. Clearly this channel between SWA and its customers is an effective way to drive revenue.

If the people who manage the voice get it right, they create a positive impact for the organization.

At the same time, an employee can make a single comment and injure the organization's relationship with everyone. Maybe because these channels of conversation are so new, many people seem to forget the volume and reach they represent. If an organization has 100,000 followers, the actual reach is much greater because if something posted is really good or really bad, many followers will forward the information or comments to their contacts. So potentially the number of people who could "hear" about it could be one million or more.

Because the responsibility is so great on those who post on behalf of the organization, it makes sense to have rules and reviews in place so

PRESIDENT OBAMA AND THE TWITTER GAFFE

FOR EXAMPLE President Obama has been a great advocate of social tools and was able to sign up more than one million followers on Twitter during the election. Within a year of being in office he had more than three million people following the office of the President through daily tweets. While on a visit to China a young girl asked him how he liked Twitter, and he responded that he'd actually never used it. There was a backlash from the press who felt betrayed because the wording of some tweets seemed to imply that the President was writing them himself. When this story got out publicly, it was delivered to many more people than the original three million followers.

costly mistakes are avoided. The first step is to make sure you're aware of anyone who reports to you who creates content for one of the organizational voice channels. You should provide specific assistance for these folks. It makes sense to review these concepts and provide training for all your people so that no one finds out the hard way the dangers of a misstep.

The Authority to Speak

The first thing your people need to understand about using social tools to communicate with the public on the organization's behalf is what authority they have and don't have. This is a basic concept, yet people will often feel they are "allowed" to respond to a negative comment they see online about the organization or one of your products. The danger here is saying something like this: "I work for X and take exception to your comment about our product. The truth is our product works exactly as specified in the instructions and if you're having that problem, it might be user error." To your employee this might sound like a reasonable response. One problem with that is if the customer learns the product was actually defective, he or she may document the story and your response, then use it as an example of how arrogant and uncaring your company is.

When television, radio, magazines, and newspapers were the main way an organization talked to the world, it was easy to restrict who could comment on your behalf. The lines of authority were clear. It's now more complicated because *every* employee has the ability to see a comment made about the organization *and to respond* in an instant to millions of people.

You must make it clear to your staff which employees are allowed to speak on behalf of the organization, and the rest are not. You must also make it clear to people how to represent themselves if they enter a conversation. The options include telling people they work for the organization and what their title is, or they can state that this is a personal opinion and not provide the organization they work for. Both of these may be more appropriate than speaking as if they're speaking for the company. You must make sure that your people understand there's a concept of authority around what they say publicly on behalf of the organization.

The Tone, Style, and Feel

For those authorized to speak on behalf of the organization, the skill of "talking" to people in the correct voice becomes important. We've now moved into a time when people are tired of and jaded by corporate speak. They want even large institutions to have a soul, and they judge that by their actions and the vernacular used when they talk to their constituents.

 KEY TERM

Corporate Speak Refers to a style of communicating that is devoid of humanness. It lacks any sense of humor, edge, or style. It's bland copy that would never offend anyone, and has been stripped of anything that would give you a sense that a human wrote it. Corporate speak often uses an overkill of industry buzzwords so that anyone reading it from outside the industry would need a dictionary to decipher the text.

There are a few difficulties in creating a consistent voice that accurately represents a brand and the organizational culture. When people are asked to write in a style that's not corporate speak, they often resort to their own personal style, and this may conflict with the specific organizational style.

To get everyone on the same page, you must be able to define how the voice should sound. Do this by showing people examples of communications that hit the mark, and combining that with descriptions of the unique elements of the voice. For example, if you look at the voice that Google uses to speak to the world, they clearly want the company to have a feel that includes a sense of humor, cleverness, openness, and a willingness to get along with other organizations and standards in the world. If you can't define how the voice should sound, people will create their own versions and that will be a branding nightmare.

Most entities have a good idea of how their voice should sound. There is a culture and history that dictates the boundaries of the voice. In some cases the voice represents the founder or current leader. If your company doesn't have a clear voice because the concept hasn't been discussed and agreed on, then stop here and direct a collective agreement on what the voice should sound and feel like for readers. Your peers will be impressed that you're raising the topic, and you'll have saved the organization from thrashing around without a coordinated feel in the communications

---

DOCUMENTING THE VOICE FRAMEWORK

The best way to get everyone on the same page when it comes to the style and tone you want to portray is to document the aspects of that voice. This document should contain descriptive words that paint a picture of what the voice should sound like (funny, serious, intelligent, professional, dynamic, artistic, etc.). It's also helpful to include samples of written text that show the style well, and samples that are clearly not the right tone.

TRICKS OF THE TRADE

---

stream. Besides, you can't go on to the next step without having the framework of a voice identified!

Training and Practice

Like any new skill that comes into being, using social tools to speak on behalf of the company is an area where virtually no one is providing training or giving people the chance to practice. In view of the consequences of getting this right or wrong, it would be wise for you to take the responsibility for helping those who work for you who might be a spokesperson. This can easily be done by providing training on how to represent the style of the organization and how to configure powerful recipes of information for your followers.

Practice creating content and conversations would seem to be a natural, but most people are thrown into the deep end to produce these communications. You can help a content producer by giving him or her a series of scenarios to respond to and let him or her practice getting the tone and style right. By providing an outside eye, you can give the producer advice on how to tweak things so that he or she can blend the content into the overall style.

Don't make the mistake of letting people dive in live. If you experiment on your constituents, you'll find out the hard way that a few days of practice might have been a good idea.

INTERNAL BEFORE EXTERNAL

TRICKS OF THE TRADE

A helpful idea is to let people practice writing in the style of the organizational voice internally before they write externally. Many companies provide content distribution through internal newsletters, blogs, or short messaging. Have people take plain content and put it into the voice for employees first, and when they're ready to go public, let them loose.

Creating Social Stars

As with any skill, some people will excel at being a content provider and surrogate voice for the organization. These social stars will develop an innate sense for the recipe of information your constituents want to hear and the tone of voice that's perfect for representing your organization. This is a new and valuable skill that must be nurtured. It's a good idea to keep your eyes open for the people who might have the right combination of skills to become social stars.

Typically, you'll find that this person must have a combination of industry knowledge, the ability to write well, empathy for your constituents, and a good sense of what content will be interesting and valuable. This person will combine all of this with a clear understanding of how social tools work. This can result in a growing network of people connected to your information channels.

Once you've found a social star, it's important to leverage his or her talents quickly and deeply because every constituent he or she helps connect to the organization is a potential new customer. The thing that excites social stars the most is being able to nurture online relationships with many people. What they want and what the organization needs are usually the same thing—a large audience participating in the conversation.

What Has History Taught Us So Far?

Over the last two years we've seen organizations go from zero to hero, while a few have shot themselves in the foot. We can learn from observing the positive and negative incidents so far. Because benefits or damage can happen so quickly when speaking to a large number of people, it's critical to have safeguards and rules in place. Not only can the organization's reputation be injured, the employee who misspoke or mishandled the situation could lose his or her job. With consequences that can accrue so quickly and at this level of seriousness, you have your work cut out for you in guiding the team through this minefield.

We live in a time when many small companies bring their products to market exclusively using social tech tools and conversations. They can reach literally billions of potential customers for free. And they can maintain an ongoing relationship by connecting through social information channels. Large organizations now have the free capability to "talk" to their customers, clients, members, and others on a daily basis. Before social technology, there was no way they could afford to talk to thousands or millions of customers every day. What we have is a completely new dynamic.

FREQUENCY OF CONTACT

MISTAKE PROOFING

If you're in the situation where you're managing some form of a social organizational voice, be careful about how often you send content. The good side of "talking" to your followers daily is they think of you often. The downside can be that you annoy them because you don't have interesting things to say each time. Don't wear out your connections by inundating them with information they won't value.

Further, large organizations can handle conversations in a way that communicates a personality and feel to people who previously thought of them as a large bureaucracy. This humanizes large organizations. People feel more comfortable talking to them, as well as buying their products. It's clear: organizations that learn to provide a valuable stream of information and conversation to followers *earn the right* to include marketing information every once in a while. This is an inexpensive way to drive revenue when you get it right.

At the same time, history shows us that organizations that don't create valuable channels of information often find that others create channels for them. In other words, a non-caring party creates discussion platforms where the company often finds it's not looked on positively. We also have seen many examples of companies that have produced

EARNING THE RIGHT TO SELL

SMART

MANAGING

We've mentioned this concept a couple of times. Almost every organization is trying to sell something. In the zeal to accomplish this, many pollute their conversation streams with too many attempts to coerce someone into taking action. Focus on providing a valuable stream of information to your constituents, and once that is accomplished, they won't mind if you sell to them every once in a while. It's akin to a television show running commercials. We don't like them all the time but we understand they fund the making of the shows.

content or made comments that came back to haunt them. We've witnessed rogue employees who have used their titles and company names while engaging in negative rants that reflected poorly on both parties.

Even though the history of the socially augmented organizational voice has been short, it has also been lively.

High Expectations

Keep in mind that there's a high expectation level when an organization speaks. This includes high expectations that the writing is high level, the spelling is correct, and the grammar is within the bounds of a college English course. People expect the content to be vetted for accuracy, and that answers are provided promptly. Everything posted is a reflection of the brand so it's never wise to be sloppy. In fact, the larger your organization, the more expectations are raised.

When we talk about social relevancy and online reputations, understand that your organizational voice is a large part of how you're perceived. For most people, this is the major way they'll interact with you. They might do a few transactions with your operation each year, but they'll read your missives and comment back to you many times a month in some cases.

> **TRICKS OF THE TRADE**
>
> ### ONE MILLION READERS
>
> A discipline that will help your people is the notion that everything they post should be looked at through the lens of one million readers. This means asking yourself before you hit Submit if the content you're about to send is professional enough to be sent to one million people. The reality is that it could possibly be read by many more, depending on the circumstances.

These high expectations need to be transferred to your people. They need to understand the responsibility they take on when they speak on behalf of the organization with social tools. Some make the mistake of thinking that the content they're posting is good enough when actually it's less than what people expect from your organization.

The Rules of the Voice

When you step back and view the short history of organizations' experiences using social tools to talk to the world, it's clear that the following set of rules can make all the difference. Keep these in mind when you speak on behalf of the organization, and when you train your people.

UNANTICIPATED PUBLICITY
Michael Arrington publishes a blog called TechCrunch. The readership is in the millions and Michael isn't opposed to reprinting information he sees published by companies large and small. This is a good example of a situation where a small tech company might post a pithy blog about a competitor they assume will only be seen by their handful of followers. Surprise, you have just been featured on TechCrunch and your image will never be the same.

1. Write like a human would speak. Corporate speak will bore people and they'll dismiss your conversation stream as a waste of time.

2. Deliver a recipe of information that's valuable to the reader. If you spend too much time trying to sell people products, you'll be regarded as spam.

3. Be ready to interact with people who comment or reply to you. The worst thing you can do is connect with people and then not answer their comments or questions.

4. Don't be a lurker. Engage in conversations when people are talking about you and your products. But only if you have something meaningful to add.

5. Have a sense of humor. Nothing makes information more interesting or seem more human than having a little fun with things.

6. Don't whine or complain. Someone is going to say something negative about your organization at some point. If you choose to engage them, do so professionally. Admit you're wrong if you are, then apologize. Or correct them if they're mistaken.

HAND OUT THESE RULES SMART
Provide a copy of these rules to anyone who might ever speak to the public using social tools. If you lead a marketing or corporate communications department, print them out poster size and put them on the wall!
MANAGING

7. Don't spin the truth, tell lies of omission, or flat out lie. This seems obvious, but do this in front of several million people, and someone will find out and tell the rest of the world.

8. Stay consistent with the tone and style of the organizational voice. It confuses and annoys people if it changes every week.

9. Never engage in flame wars with competitors or angry constituents. This makes everyone look immature.

10. If you don't have anything valuable to say, don't say anything at all. It's better to be silent than obviously filling space because you feel you should. By the way, go find something valuable to say!

Manager's Checklist for Chapter 8

☑ New social and Internet capabilities let the organization talk to constituents. Managers are critical in ensuring this capability is used properly.

☑ Recognize when a process involves this voice and put controls in place to maximize the positive and minimize the dangers.

☑ Respect the fact that this new capability is public, permanent, and not a place to be sloppy. Controls must be in place to assure that top quality content is provided every time it's used.

☑ There are best practices proven to make this new capability a positive, and you need to take responsibility for teaching your people about them.

☑ Understand what the organizational voice sounds like when it comes to tone, style, and feel, and make sure that everyone who posts content is consistent with how it will be interpreted by the reader (listener).

☑ Always be on the lookout for the potential social stars who are great at representing the organization in the social sphere, and leverage their abilities.

☑ Document the boundaries, goals, voice, style, and tone so that anyone who speaks on behalf of the organization is clear on what you want to accomplish.

Social Tools and Virtual Teams

Most people seem to first think of social technologies as tools used for external marketing and advertising, when the truth is the volume of usage is probably more internal to organizations. The majority of case studies and stories in the traditional press concern businesses that are driving revenue and relationships with customers through Facebook, blogs, or Twitter. If we could see the overall use of social tools on some kind of color-coded infographic, where one color was front-end marketing and networking applications and the other color was internal use, we might be surprised at what we'd see.

This is much like the area of computer security where outside hackers get most of the press, when it's actually the internal security breaches that far outweigh attacks from outside. We spend more time communicating with the people we work with when compared to people outside the organization. This is an important distinction. You need to be aware that if you're managing a team involved in the organization's back office, you still have many valuable uses for social tech tools. So that leads us to a discussion of another high-value area for using social tools and that's their application within virtual teams.

There's been a quiet shift in how many people perform their jobs over the last 20 years or so. We're moving away from the model where the majority of knowledge workers reported to one location and worked with a team of people in the same building. We're moving toward a model where more people are working from their homes, remote offices, or contracting out their services as freelancers. Even within large organizations with lots of people and many buildings, we see the formation of teams that cross geography so people aren't physically working with others on their team.

Although there are economic and business reasons why this change in work structure makes sense, the catalyst is technology. The Internet provided the first leap forward because it allowed people to connect to corporate servers more easily, so working from home was a step simpler. E-mail became common and this provided a free, efficient way for people to communicate across the hall or around the world. Then new Web-based communication tools like instant messaging and Skype went a step further and allowed people to communicate over distance as if someone were sitting next to them—again, for free.

Quickly following these communication advances, we developed portals and collaborative workspaces online so that teams could share resources and information with the click of a button. The easier it became to communicate and collaborate, the less sense it made to make everyone report physically to the same place at the same time. We also were freed from being forced to create a team out of people who happened

> **SMART MANAGING**
>
> **INTERNAL SOCIAL TECH USAGE**
>
> This is important. Social tools can be put to work in accounting, HR, operations, and product development departments with the same value they can be used in marketing and advertising. Be sure to note how concepts like crowdsourcing, collaboration tools, and virtual team support can be applied with value to any backoffice operation.

> **FOR EXAMPLE**
>
> **OUTSOURCING ENABLED**
>
> One obvious example of technology supporting virtual teams is the concept of outsourcing. Once companies realized they could get simple, repetitive tasks done more cheaply overseas and that technology would provide the infrastructure to support this, they were free to lower costs by negotiating low labor rates in other places. This never would have been practical without technology.

to live in the same city. We could create teams from the best talent we could find, regardless of where they lived or what hours they worked. All of this has now added up to a new paradigm—the virtual team.

Now there's a second-generation technology-based push to enable even more use of remote workers and virtual teams, and that comes from the ability to use social technologies to collaborate and manage teams. Social tools are by nature communication and collaboration platforms. That makes them invaluable in supporting the move toward virtual teams. For this reason, it's critical that you understand how to leverage social tools to enable your virtual employees to work well and to aid you in your management duties. As

THE UNPLANNED IMPACT OF CELL PHONES

FOR EXAMPLE

It's possible that the cell phone may have been one of the most powerful enablers of working remotely because it allowed people to be available wherever and whenever someone else on the team needed them. Once we weren't tethered to our desks for people to find us, the need for the desk, the office, the building, then coordinating workers' hours, went away.

with any other tool, you can use social tech in many ways to augment virtual teams, or they can be misused and cripple the situation.

Why Virtual Teams Make Sense

Like most fundamental changes in how organizations operate, there are cultural and profit drivers behind why we're moving toward a more dispersed workforce. For many managers, this happened slowly and without a lot of planning or thought. The problem is we haven't invested much time or energy learning how to manage virtual teams well. So here we are, just now understanding that they're a different animal from geo-located teams. How did we move from teams in cube farms to a dispersed model so quickly? The following dynamics have had a lot to do with it:

- The number of women in the workforce grew substantially after World War II. This led to them assuming important roles in the organization and at the same time dealing with raising children. Because their work product was so valued, employers often tried to find ways to let them operate from home yet remain connected to the office.

■ At the same time, people became more mobile and interested in moving to different locations. In some cases, organizations didn't want to lose a top performer so they made allowances and let them work from whatever city they chose to move to.

■ At various times over the last couple decades, the economy has turned down and organizations have been forced to look toward cutting expenses. Buildings and offices are a huge expense so allowing people to work from home actually saved organizations money.

■ In many cities the commute to work was beginning to take hours of time. People were literally spending almost 20 percent of their workday just getting to and from the office. If the worker was able to perform their duties from home, they were able to reinvest some of that travel time in work hours and be more productive.

■ As companies experimented with outsourcing, they learned that an expert anywhere in the world could often be inserted into a team to fill a specific role for a finite time.

■ People began to realize that with cell phones and Internet connections they were able to be productive wherever they happened to be. When that reality set in, the need to be in the office diminished. Once that stranglehold was broken, people began to look at options for staying on a team, but not having to be local all the time.

When you combine organizations being able to hold on to good workers even when they couldn't be in the office and the cost savings they realized plus the performance benefits of finding the best workers regardless of location, you have clear motivation to change. From the workers' standpoint, remote working and virtual teams mean more flexibility in where you live, where you work, and when you work. This is a winner for the staff. Since both sides of the equation like the dynamics, you can see why we're inching in this direction.

The negative in this trend comes when you're the one who has to manage people who don't sit a stone's throw from you. The organization may be happy and workers may be happy, but you're the one who needs to create a sense of teamwork across a group that may have never met in person. You're the one who must keep projects running on time when they're split up among people all over the Earth. You're the one who must

IS THERE REALLY A PRODUCTIVITY ADVANTAGE?

Amid the euphoria everyone is feeling about how nicely virtual teams and remote working are fitting into our lives, there's a seed of doubt. There's actually been little research into the real productivity gains and losses of having dispersed teams. Unless you're a very savvy manager who feels comfortable running virtual teams, you might find that they're not as fruitful as your leadership would like to believe. The gains may be offset by the difficulties in getting people to trust each other and work seamlessly when not on site.

CAUTION

counsel and coach employees over the wire because there's no other option. In short, you're the one stuck with the hard part! Not to worry—we discuss some best practices for managing virtual teams later in this chapter. You have something else working in your favor, and that's the fire hose of some innovative social tech applications.

How Technology is Enabling This Revolution

When the economy was primarily manufacturing based, people had to be at the factory because there was a production line and tools on site to get things built. Spin forward and we have a knowledge-based economy where the majority of jobs are performed through conversations or time in front of a computer screen. Every day we lose more manufacturing jobs to robotic assembly systems and outsourcing to other countries. Especially in the United States today, a large percentage of careers are knowledge based and don't require a worker to be on site.

Technology has been steadily infiltrating our organizations, careers, and lives for the last 30 years. It's been a catalyst in this virtual team paradigm in a number of ways. In the early 1980s with the advent of the personal computer, technology became more portable. Ergo, we could take it home with us, unlike the mainframe terminals before. With the Internet, it became simpler to connect, communicate, and share resources online. With

YAMMER.COM

One new tool virtual teams can use to communicate with each other in real time is Yammer. This private chat service acts like a combination of Twitter and a discussion group so that members of a team can share information or conversations with the entire group at once.

TOOLS

social tools, we have even more sophisticated options for communicating and working collaboratively in real time. Every new stage of computing progress frees us from location-based working.

Technologies that provide groups of people the ability to manage projects together have been merged with eCommunity tools so that a virtual team has visibility into all the task lists and results provided by each person. This category of social tools has been a boon for managers because it solves the problem of a disparate team not knowing the progress of others, and provides a single place for you to go to judge whether projects are on track.

BASECAMP

Basecamp (http://basecamphq .com) is a great example of a collaborative Web site used by virtual teams to manage projects and share resources. If you're responsible for managing projects across people who don't work in the same place, tools like this are invaluable.

TOOLS

Although the cell phone has been a critical element in facilitating the ability to reach anyone, anywhere, anytime, the ultimate form of communication is having a video call with someone anytime and from anywhere. As human beings, we're more comfortable understanding what someone is really saying when we see the person face-to-face.

Think about this concept as a continuum of intimacy in communication tools. At one end is text messaging, with its short quick vocabulary and a real difficulty in expressing emotions or complicated information. E-mail would be next, and it solves the ability to send complicated information because we have more room for words, but the context and emotions behind the words can be easily misconstrued. Then comes the phone, and this at least allows for voice inflection so that we can discern how someone feels. The next step is video calls, or conferencing, and finally in-person communication. Apple has now provided a slick ability to do connect-with-video over its new iPhone, so we can assume that in the near future, it will be a normal thing to talk face-to-face over our mobile device.

Technology has provided the ability to do group-based video conferencing by using vendors like Cisco and Polycom, or person-to-person with free tools like Skype. The only problem is group-based can be expensive, and person-to-person can be low quality, depending on your equipment. However, we're standing on the precipice of very high quality video calls—for free. This will further enable people to move toward the virtual team concept.

What Does This Mean for You?

As mentioned earlier, the most difficult aspect of the virtual team and remote worker concept is how to manage people and build a frictionless team when people aren't physically together. The dynamics of team building and managing people are different when they can't interact in person. You don't have the ability to build trust and a bond through people having lunches together, talking in the breakroom, and building personal relationships away from work.

Virtual team members don't have as much visibility into how others operate or what their backgrounds are, and this can lead to lack of trust. You're forced into situations where you must have crucial conversations with team members about their performance over the wire instead of in person, and this can sometimes cause awkwardness. Managing virtually is not optimum and will never be as productive as a face-to-face interaction, yet with no choice, you'll have to do this the best you can. The critical thing for you to note is that managing people virtually is a unique skill and is different than managing people within arm's reach.

To further complicate matters, employees of different generations have varying levels of comfort with technology. That causes issues when some team members are great at using collaboration tools, while others refuse to use them. The same thing holds true with communication tools.

MANAGING OVER THE WIRE

CAUTION

When you need to have a crucial conversation with an employee, and there's no option for bringing the person into the office, don't use e-mail as a substitute. This is the perfect situation to use a video call so that you're as close to face-to-face as possible. It might seem efficient to fire off an e-mail, or even just to pick up the phone, but looking someone in the eyes still helps set the right tone. Whatever you do, don't text someone to say he or she did something wrong!

When 75 percent of the team is comfortable using video conferencing as a way to meet, but 25 percent refuse to play, it becomes awkward at best when the team meets. You'll have to play the role of trainer and inspirational leader to get people to use the tools the team has standardized on.

You also have to be instrumental in choosing (demanding, in some cases) the technology tools the team will use. Then you'll have to be the lead example of how to use them, because everyone will watch you to see how you use the tools. If you choose a collaboration platform and then fail to use it, no one else will either.

There's no magic formula for being a great virtual team manager. To be effective you need to learn a collection of new skills, and adhere to a few dos and don'ts that will make the difference.

Handling the Challenges of Managing a Virtual Team

The first thing you need to understand is how different it is to manage virtually, and what the issues are. Once you understand the areas of difficulty, you can work to improve them. For many managers, the unique issues of managing remote workers are not something they've given much thought to. They slowly, over time, went from managing people who all worked together, to managing people who are spread all over. They never stopped to think about the difference in dynamics and the consequent leadership needs. It's a *very* different challenge, and it takes a new set of skills.

Social technologies are giving us some wonderful tools to help virtual teams and remote workers tie even tighter to their office-bound mates, yet technology is only an enabler of how people interact. On its own, it can't make all the friction points go away.

> **SPATIAL AWARENESS**   **SMART MANAGING**
>
> Before you go any further, survey the people who report to you and identify what percent are location-based and what percent are remote. Think about the remote workers and the challenges you've had with them. If you have a majority who are remote, take notes on this section. If not, read this for future reference.

Let's look at a few of the trouble spots you might already be seeing with your teams.

Relationship Building

When we raise the topic of relationship building within a virtual team, we mean building relationships among the employees on the team, and between you and the team. Employees need to trust each other to get high-quality work done on time, and they need to be ready to help each other out when needed. They also need to trust you, and that doesn't always come easily to people who have only "met" you through a Skype call. Trust and healthy relationships are elements that have to be built and earned. They don't happen because you demand it, and they don't come quickly. That said, there are some things you can do to speed up the process.

One thing to remember is that you need your people to *trust you first* before they build trust in each other, and if you're remote from a team member, that will be harder to do. The worst case is when you manage a team of people who all work together physically, but you manage from afar! They aren't around you enough to see how you handle yourself or how you would interact with them in person every day. Since trust is built through experiences, you have a harder time earning it because the volume of experiences is less when you don't pass each other in the halls. The best way to counter this is to be available and to establish a consistent rhythm of when you communicate with them. If they trust you as the leader, they will at least fly in the formation you set even if they don't know about the person next to them.

Trust is also built because you do as you say. This means you lead by example, and in the virtual world that includes using the technologies you ask your people to use. One of the worst things you can do is to require them to use communication and collaboration tools that you don't use yourself.

ASSUMING YOU HAVE TRUST

One of the downsides about a relationship primarily conducted over Web-based communication tools is that trust is often assumed, when in reality there is none. This is true whether you're chatting with someone you met on Match.com or e-mailing someone who reports to you. Even though you're the person's boss, don't assume the person trusts you. You earn trust through repeated actions that form a pattern.

CAUTION

Communication Rhythm Refers to the frequency and consistency of the times that people communicate. When the timing of communication methods becomes predictable, they fall into a comfortable rhythm and people come to trust and know they can count on the information exchange and networking.

KEY TERM

This may seem like a little thing, but doing video calls with people every few days instead of a voice call makes a big different in trust levels. When people see your face, that makes you seem real to them as opposed to a disembodied voice from beyond that calls to check up on them. Take the time to use tools like Skype or FaceTime (iPhone) and schedule video calls regularly, even when it seems harder than picking up the phone.

To foster trust among virtual team members who may have never met in person, you need to handle things differently. The rhythm of team meetings now becomes important because the team needs to know they'll be meeting regularly. This helps show them that everyone on the team is engaged and getting their work done. The more they can verify that the people they're teamed with are upstanding citizens, the more they feel led to perform well themselves. The alternative to having a good rhythm of meetings is that there are long spaces in between. In that space, people naturally question whether things are getting done by others, and this de-motivates people and lowers their trust in the team.

The agenda for remote meetings must include everyone updating the others on his or her progress. Hearing people verbalize their progress and, even better, seeing them talk, helps them get to know the styles of others. To the extent that some people hang back in meetings without ever updating the team, the others will consider the nonparticipants as nonexistent. It's not possible to maintain a tight level of trust if some members skip a meeting and people are told to e-mail their progress to the boss. Team members need to be proud when they've done well, admit when they're behind, and ask for help when it's needed—and all while communicating to the group.

You must be conscious of the natural distrust that exists for the skills and work ethic of the team members you don't see every day or hear from regularly. Out of sight can become out of mind, and that's not good for team dynamics. Using technology to facilitate visibility and conversations remotely helps solve this potential hurdle.

Project Management

There are many online project management systems that allow remote teams of people to collaborate in real time. Group project management is one of the hardest types of

> **BREAK UP TASKS**
> *TRICKS OF THE TRADE*
>
> An effective change you can make when managing a virtual team is to break up tasks into smaller pieces so that people complete them faster, and get the reward of saying they're done with a piece. This also ensures that people don't take on long projects and the first time you hear there's a problem (because you can't see them work) is when they tell you they're going to miss a deadline.

disciplines to deal with when you're trying to complete a complicated project. An application like Basecamp coordinates what tasks are assigned to whom, and what the timeline is for completion. It also provides methods for sharing resources that might be useful to everyone (documents, spreadsheets, graphics, videos, etc.). One thing to keep in mind is that collaboration tools like this can help with the mechanical management of a project, but they do nothing to inspire and encourage people. Nor do they sort out conflicts among team members.

Problems like these need to be solved by you personally. When you sense there's conflict between people on a project or that the will to go forward is lagging, you have to jump in and manage things. This is a perfect time to use video-conferencing tools to get your message across effectively or to sort out disagreements. This is also where you can use group discussion tools like Yammer so that you can constantly pump up people and be aware of conflict that might be brewing.

Personality Styles

It comes as no surprise to you as a manager that personality conflicts may cause some problems when leading a virtual team. Personality differences are one of the major causes of issues in a team whether team members work in the same place or not, and they're magnified when people work remotely.

Here's an example of how social tools and personality profiles intersect. Joe and Roxanne are on a team of developers that's building a software

SMART

PERSONALITY PROFILING

We urge you to invest some time and money in personality profiling of team members if you're running a virtual team. There are lots of options, like DiSC and Meyers-Briggs. Once you have a clear picture as to what drives people, it's easier to keep relationships running smoothly.

MANAGING

application for a large bank. Joe works from home and Roxanne from a company office across the country. Joe is a strong introvert and Roxanne is an extrovert.

This shows up in the use of technology and communication styles in that Joe goes dark for days at a time while he writes code day and night. He has no interest in jumping online to chat or updating the project management system. He prefers e-mail as a communication form because it's convenient and keeps others from wasting his time talking. Joe likes to be alone, concentrate, and work in long hard sessions.

Because Roxanne is an extrovert, she needs people to inspire her. She wants to hear others' ideas, she needs input, and she needs community. Discussions give her the energy to do her programming, and when she's alone in her office, she wears down staring at a computer screen. She likes to write code in short bursts, spread out over 14 hours, and wants to check her progress with Joe and the others constantly. She regularly updates the online project management system so she can let others know what she's done and check in on what they've done. She tries to Skype Joe and others at least five times a day to kick around ideas and progress.

You can see where this is going. After a few months of working together, both parties annoy the other with their use of technology tools and their specific styles. As a savvy manager, you know how to help them come to some agreement on what communication technologies to use and when. You also help them broker a way to work together that's acceptable to both—right? Neither personality style is right or wrong. They both have strengths and weaknesses. The art in managing people is learning to create harmony by leveraging the strengths of both.

The more you're faced with managing remotely, the more you'll notice how important technology tools are in keeping things running smoothly. At the same time, the more you'll notice that personality styles and generational differences cause people to utilize these tools in productive ways or not at all. Recognizing the problem is the first step to the solution. Make sure you pick the right social and technology tools to support your team, and then help everyone learn to use them in the right ways—regardless of their proclivity to use them.

Technology has done a great job of helping us move to this virtual team–remote worker model. Social tech has

AVOIDANCE IS EASIER THAN REPAIR

SMART MANAGING

One of the most important reasons to understand personality styles is to assure that they don't cause conflicts. Virtual team disagreements are much harder to sort out. When people get sideways with each other in person, you can sit down, talk it out, shake hands, and move on. You can't do this online as easily. You also don't have the visibility to see if someone is ready to move on. If the person isn't ready and works remotely, his or her performance may drop steeply and you won't know this for some time.

given us a new toolbox full of communication and collaboration tools. You must learn how to apply these to help your virtual team work frictionlessly. You also have to help them learn how to use these tools in ways acceptable to each person. It's unwise to assume you can assemble a team of professionals, toss in a few technology tools, and out pops a well-oiled machine. You have to work harder as a leader to keep things on track and be even more careful about the technology tool use if you want things to go well.

What the Future Holds

An interesting thing to consider is where we might be headed with virtual teams. Will working remotely become more prevalent than it is today? Will a vast amount of the workforce be allowed to work from home? Will flexible scheduling become the norm? There are good arguments that the catalysts that have been driving the current trends aren't played out. For example, organizations will continue to look for ways to cut costs and raise productivity. If people are asked to work harder and longer hours, they're going to want more say over where they work and when so they can fit in a personal life.

The technologies that have been urging virtual teams forward are only going to get better. Companies like Cisco are spending millions of dollars

KEY TERM — **Telepresence** Refers to systems that use flat panel monitors and cameras arranged around a table so that the people who are remote appear to be sitting at the table. The people who are remote can see everyone else at the table in the same way so it's like everyone is "present."

to promote and refine their telepresence systems so people appear to be on site during meetings. New applications that extend services like Face-Time, which can stream video cheaply and in high quality from any mobile device, make it easier to talk face-to-face from any two points in the world. New collaboration tools will make it easier to see the work others are doing in real time, and to literally work on the same document, video, or picture at the same time. In fact, there's no question that virtual meeting rooms will become the standard way for remote teams to meet.

The trends seem to support a future where there are more remote workers and virtual teams, and in fact they may become the majority of the workforce. If this happens, the specific management skills and technology knowledge needed to lead a virtual workforce will be in great demand.

New Combinations of Players

Another possibility is that virtual teams will begin to add members who are freelancers, contractors, and possibly even anonymous. As crowd-sourcing and freelance contracting Web sites become more trusted, organizations may look at a specific team role as something of a commodity, and therefore feel comfortable having a remote contractor or an anonymous worker from the Web crowd fill a role.

Imagine if we get to the point where a graphic designer is a commodity job and we really don't need to know your name or where you're from, only that you can design a Web screen and that you'll charge $50 an hour. We can engage you for 60 days, then let you go when the project is done. No termination, no institutional memory issues, no hard feelings.

What if roles within large companies become like standard plug-and-play positions where the skills are defined and known? Teams could be assembled based on skill sets and availability, with technology underpinning the coordination and communication among people regardless if they're on the "payroll." In this case, ad hoc teams can be pulled together for a project and locked into a set of technology tools. They perform, they complete, and they disband and move on to the next project.

TECHNOLOGISTS

Some people would say that this model is already happening in the technology space. In cloud computing operations there are security specialists, network engineers, developers, cablers, and help desk people. We are starting to look at these workers as pieces of a puzzle, where clients rent their talents and in many cases have no idea what their names are.

Virtual Management Specialists

If the world continues to move in this direction, we'll see managers who specialize in building and running virtual teams. These brave souls may be on staff or could be contractors, and will be brought in on a project-by-project basis because of their specific talent for knowing how to use technology tools and remote leadership skills to get results.

Take a minute and think about your specific skills and talents. Ponder whether you're a leader who works better with a team that sits within sight or one who has the unique combination of skills that could help you stand out as we move more toward a virtual world. Do you have a strong command of the inventory of social and technology tools that can be applied to help build trust and relationships and manage projects across distances? Do you have a strong sense of personality styles and how to get them to blend? Do you have the ability to inspire and motivate people over the wire? If you do, you might think about moving toward a specific skill in running virtual teams and remote workforces because it appears they're here to stay, and growing.

Know that you now have a powerful set of tools that you can leverage to improve your ability to manage remote workers and virtual teams. Add to this the unique skills of a manager who is required to lead a virtual team, and you have a higher value to whatever organization you're employed by. This is also known as a good career move!

Manager's Checklist for Chapter 9

☑ Virtual teams as a concept are growing, and you need to learn the special skills necessary to assemble and manage them well.

☑ Technology tools provide a powerful solution to many of the inherent problems with virtual teams. There's a good inventory of technology that every manager must be aware of that can bring a virtual team together. Having first-hand knowledge of these tools is critical to managing well.

☑ You can use technology to help people communicate more effectively, collaborate in real time, and build relationships more quickly. All of this builds trust among team members and that's critical in remote environments.

☑ Getting people to adopt the virtual team tools quickly and uniformly is difficult, and the manager must work hard to get this done. People may adopt these tools at different rates based on personality type or age demographic.

☑ The drivers of the virtual team and remote worker paradigm continue to expand.

☑ Managers may one day become specialists in either onsite or virtual management, and will be assigned exclusively one way or the other.

Managing Social Tech by the Numbers

A s a manager, you've surely noticed that it helps to have a framework to guide people to a destination and measurements that help them understand their progress. Goals set a concise end state or level of achievement that you want your team to acquire. Measurements and analytics help them understand the dynamics that influence their odds of success or point to the reasons for missing the target. It's not difficult in most cases to identify the drivers of success and provide measurements for them so everyone can see the formula for reaching the goal. Yet too many managers and people in general avoid measuring progress, either out of fear of what they might see or a lack of understanding of the value.

What experienced managers know is that setting goals and then measuring the progress is the surest way to success. If you want to be a star in implementing social tech, you have to apply these principles to be able to dream up new uses, set targets, and then reach them as soon as possible. Along the way you'll surely be asked to defend your investment of resources in social concepts, so learning to measure the ROI (return on investment) or ROE (return on effort) will be important.

There are lots of blog posts these days discussing measurement of social tech. The hottest topic is whether organizations are getting a return on investment or simply following the herd on another technology goose

> **Return on Investment/Effort** A common phrase people talk about is ROI, or return on investment. Another measurement we use in this book is return on effort (ROE). Both terms
> **KEY TERM** refer to the likelihood that you'll receive more value from results than the resources you invested in a particular area. An example would be if you put five hours into using Twitter each week, do you get value back that would equal the value of the time you invested, or are you wasting time you could be using elsewhere?

chase. Social tech is such an amorphous practice that it can be difficult to control it, leverage it, or figure out the value it might be providing. To manage anything well, you must be able to quantify the investment and the return. Absent this, you're flying blind and have little idea how improvements can be made or where problems might be cropping up.

On the other hand, there are some people who say social tech is a tool and we don't always measure the value of tools. We don't always set goals for tool proficiency. Do we measure the value of Microsoft Office? Do we measure the value of the Internet? How about the value of e-mail? Do we ever set goals as to the skill levels with using any of these tools? We just assume that the technologies are valuable and that their worth is self-evident. Can't we do the same with social tools?

Our answer to that is there's no question that technologies can eventually become so standard we cease to measure whether they have value; we just assume it. We might not measure the value of Internet usage in general, but we do measure Web site traffic. We also might measure the amount of time that employees spend using certain sites. The same dynamic applies to social tech in general. It might not be critical to measure the overall worth of social tools, but it makes sense to measure certain discreet areas that can be critical to the bottom line.

As a manager, you have the responsibility to get the best performance out of your team. This requires that you know when they're hitting the mark and when they need improvement. Social technology is a game changer in some areas of an organization, and can be helpful in the rest. Ensuring that it's used and used well is a noble goal—and the whole point of this book! So let's look at two critical outcomes that come from measuring social tech usage and impact.

What Gets Measured Gets Done

A funny thing about human beings, when someone is holding a stopwatch to us, we work faster. When we know that our performance is going to be measured, we pay a little closer attention to what we're doing and how we're measuring up. Goals drive behavior because they state clearly what needs to be done. Measurements tell us how we're doing along the path.

With new tools like social tech, there's a dual benefit to putting measurement systems and analytics in place. Not only do you get to see how things are coming along, you also put pressure on people to achieve. Since social tech is new, there are still many people who have no interest in using it or are curmudgeonly about it. Measuring social tech progress is a good way to push them along so they'll step into it and see how it might be a benefit.

During these early days of social tools, think about making it fun for people to reach their goals. Create contests for your team so that they have extra incentives to learn the tools and expand their horizons. Reward people with the most connections, the people who create the most content, or the people who have the highest social relevancy scores. You won't have to do this forever, just in the early days.

> **SOCIAL CONNECTIONS AND NETWORKING**
> FOR EXAMPLE
>
> A simple goal that you could give to people so they start coming up the curve with social tools is to set a goal for the number of connections you'd like them to have. Help them sign up for LinkedIn if they're not already, then give them a goal of connecting to at least 200 people on LinkedIn within a specified time. This is an easy task and sets you up to give them a few tasks to do using this network that shows them the value.

Never forget the concept we mentioned earlier: what gets measured gets done. Almost all of us are very task- and goal-oriented. Give us a target and we'll focus our energies to try and "win." Fail to set expectations, and we often make it a low priority.

Analyzing Results Will Show What Must Be Improved

The second byproduct of setting goals and measuring progress is that you'll see statistically where people or social campaigns are missing the mark. The use of social tools is still in the experimental stage. In some cases, learning what doesn't work is as important as learning what does.

Comparing results of team members can tell you who has developed a best practice for making something work and who needs training. Measuring variables on a new marketing campaign can yield valuable information about what pieces might work and who is struggling. This can be important because without analyzing social campaigns you might be led to believe that an entire pilot project didn't work, when it was only a small element that brought down the results.

FOR EXAMPLE

TWITTER COUPON EXAMPLE

Imagine you decide to test using Twitter as a delivery vehicle for coupons to your customers. After six months of trying it—without analyzing results—you ask around and people tell you that they don't really think it's working. This is the problem with ad hoc results. If you react to this information, you might make a serious mistake. Had you measured all the steps in your coupon program, you would have learned that your people only signed up 150 followers and when the coupons were released on Twitter you actually had a 10 percent redemption rate. The reality is the results were awesome—a 10 percent redemption rate is great. The only issue you really face is not having figured out how to sign up more people, and that can be improved greatly.

If you want to learn to use social tools faster than the competition, you must get scientific about identifying the specific activities you want to learn to do. Then be aggressive about setting goals and measuring results. The faster you learn your lessons, the faster you'll reap the benefits. This applies whether you're in sales, marketing, accounting, operations, or human resources. An analytical approach helps you identify the friction points and smooth them out.

Ideas for Areas to Measure

When it comes to measuring social tech results, there are three areas that can be measured:

- Measure the overall organization's progress in using the tools.
- Measure individual users' proficiency.
- Measure the results of a specific social campaign run by a team.

It's commonplace for organizations to have at least a few enterprise-wide social tech measurements that are being monitored. This could be the number of people who are following the company blogs or Twitter accounts. Or possibly measuring the number of mentions of the organization or its products. Some are even measuring the sentiment ratio so they know if there are more positive comments than bad. All these are valuable, but they don't replace the measurements you can use to make progress with your team and on your projects. They simply memorialize how the overall efforts are going. The social battles will be won on specific social campaigns and with specific key employees.

Personal Use Measurements

The fastest way to bring your team up the learning curve with social tools is to develop a series of goals and measurements that let them have some fun competing with each other and at the same time acquire valuable results and knowledge. Here are some examples of specific areas you could measure:

- The number of business connections on social networking sites like LinkedIn, Facebook, Twitter, or blog readers. These connections could be customers, prospects, clients, vendors, partners, or industry thought leaders.

- Amount of business content posted on social sites, blogs, Twitter, etc. The more prolific someone is with posting valuable industry or professional content, the more he or she will be viewed as an industry expert by people searching to see his or her online credentials. The more impressive your people look online, the more impressed people will be with your organization as they represent you on the Web.

- Number of times content they produce for social media sites is viewed, downloaded, or passed on to others. This is obviously the best measurement of the quality of the content. The more people who share content virally with others, the more they're putting a stamp of approval on it.

- Quality of information sources in their river of information, and volume of valuable content discovered and passed on to others on the team. Maintaining and working a powerful river of information normally translates into a high career IQ, so measuring the proficiency with this skill helps put focus on it.

■ Use of crowdsourcing tools as a way to lower costs for the organization. For some positions in the company, you could literally set targets for expense reduction by incentivizing people to use crowdsourcing as a tool to get work done fast and inexpensively.

■ If you're in the HR department, you could measure the number of recruits who were identified using social tools.

■ If you run a sales department, you could measure the number of new leads your sales people generate using social tools.

■ If you run an accounting department, you could measure the quality and volume of sources in the rivers of information your team has built.

■ If you run the marketing/PR department, you could measure the number of mentions your people get by promoting information to bloggers and twitterers.

■ If you're in customer service, you could measure the number of people you've contacted who mentioned your products negatively or positively in their blogs or tweets.

This list could go on, so look at this as simply a few examples that can be used to inspire personal success. The idea is to challenge your people to learn new skills, then apply them to tasks they may have been doing in other ways for years. Sometimes people need an extra push to use a more beneficial tool even when it's pretty clear that what they've been using isn't as effective. There are still a few carpenters who refuse to use a nail gun because they love their trusty hammer so much. And there are still a few people who have a Rolodex on their desks because they don't really understand why LinkedIn is more efficient and useful.

REWARDING CAPABILITY USAGE

One mistake managers make when putting together goals and measurements is to focus on number of connections and usage frequency instead of the broad understanding of how to use a tool. For example, they get caught up in getting their people to get the most connections they can on LinkedIn, instead of rewarding the usage of the five or six really interesting capabilities LinkedIn provides. A big network is only the first step. What you really want to measure is your people's ability to leverage that network to get things done.

Social Campaign Measurements

If you're going to produce valuable analytics on a specific social campaign, measurements are critical because you must be able to discern which pieces of the campaign worked and which didn't. A marketing campaign, for example, might have ten elements that have to come together for the overall program to work. If any one element fails, the whole program could have poor results. There's an art to putting measurement systems in place to track these elements so you know what worked and what didn't within the larger picture of "Did it drive revenue?"

Because there are many types of social campaigns that can be tested in the market, let's take a look at some examples so you get an idea of how to measure them in a useful way:

If you run a campaign to see how many people you can drive from a blog posting to your Web site by providing links in the blog, you might measure the conversion rate (percentage of people who clicked on the links). Then you could measure the conversion rate of people who went to the site who took some action. You might also measure the percentage of people who shared the link with a friend and used eWord of mouth to increase your click-throughs.

When you run a pilot project to see how much you can increase the number of people reading a blog or following a Twitter stream, you want to get a clear picture of *why* the growth happened (if it did). Let's assume you work hard to provide a great stream of information, and then take proactive steps to market the blog or Twitter stream in print pieces and provide some discount coupons that get delivered exclusively through these channels. That's three factors that could influence subscriber growth. You'd want to do these one at a time so you could test the efficacy of each channel separately, or you'll have to do some work to identify which effort drove the signups.

An interesting type of campaign being run now is an effort to generate "on demand" sales with a Twitter coupon. The idea here is that a discount can be given to Twitter followers that is time based (e.g., for the next six hours) and that they must redeem on site or with an immediate phone call. The analytics of this need to be the percentage of followers who acted on the coupon, how many of these are current customers, and how many are buying for the

SMART

MANAGING

BEING SCIENTIFIC

It's important to think scientifically when putting together analytics on social campaigns and pilot projects. You want to know *exactly* why something you're trying is working or not. What you need to know is exactly *why* you had success or not. Be careful about mixing too many tactics in one pilot project or campaign because you'll have a hard time discerning what were the drivers of success or failure. Scientists only change one variable at a time so they can accurately tell if that variable makes a difference.

first time. Then it would be wise to run discounts of varying size so you can see what the difference in redemption rate might be. By doing this scientifically, you can discover the perfect blend of discount and time offered to drive the profitability and revenue you want.

Many HR departments are building the skill of doing employment campaigns to recruit new employees using social tools. The analytics of this type of effort need to provide information on the cost differences of social recruiting versus running ads that cost money. You would also want to evaluate the speed difference in the time it takes to fill job openings and the quality levels of the prospects discovered when compared to traditional methods.

To learn how to impact your online reputation, run a pilot project to get customers to write positive mentions of your products online. This generates positive word of mouth in the social circles. The kinds of things that can be measured are the number of mentions, the percentage of customers you can give incentives to push them to speak positively about you online, and the impact of various incentives. Ultimately, you want to be able to measure whether this impacts future sales. This is hard to dis-

CAUTION

NEGATIVE RESULTS

Be careful not to let negative results be viewed as a failure when you run a campaign. Every social project you run won't be a raging success the first time. When a pilot project or social marketing campaign fails to reach the goals, take an unemotional look at why it didn't work, and re-run the effort after changing a variable that likely caused it to fail. Remember Thomas Edison and the filament experiments he did with the light bulb? He failed over 100 times and continued to experiment until he found his solution. He didn't quit even when he got frustrated because he knew he was learning everything that didn't work, and that would guide him to what did.

cover since a sales gain or loss could be caused by many things. The only way to know for sure that positive online comments help is to survey new customers and ask what spurred them to buy the products.

One of the most important measurements for any specific campaign or pilot project is the ROI or ROE. No matter how successful something is, if it cost more to make it successful than the benefit you'll get over the next 18 months, it might not be worth repeating. Think about this: you could spend $100,000 to get one million followers on Twitter and be very excited about hitting that goal. But if you don't find a way to get the return of your $100,000, that's not a great investment. Measuring and analyzing the details is great; just don't forget there needs to be a payback at some point.

Hidden Return on Investment

When evaluating ROI, understand that sometimes value is created that's hard to measure. For example, your one million Twitter followers may not turn directly into sales that you can measure, but they may be a great source of word of mouth in generating new customers you would have had a hard time identifying. Brand awareness is also hard to measure, but clearly helps a company. If you get thousands of people talking about your brand on Facebook, that will likely translate to something positive. You may not have a way to analyze this, however.

CAUTION

Measurement Tools

There are a number of free Web-based tools you can use to gather measurements. Once captured, you put them together into easy-to-understand dashboards. When you first start gathering results, you may want to put the numbers together and enter them into Excel. Just capturing and getting them into a document is helpful. As a middle step, you can use the graphics capabilities in Excel to create bar charts and pie charts if you want to get a bit more graphical. Later, there are Web tools or installed applications that take your results and turn them into literal dashboards with dials and graphs that show you at a glance how you're doing.

To gather the data to put into dashboards, you need to use an additional set of tools that can help you find the information you need on users, mentions, and sentiment levels. A number of Web sites now provide this information for free, and there are others that are more enterprise-class that help

DASHBOARD APPLICATIONS

TOOLS To try out a few advanced applications that create dashboards, try services like Quadbase.com, Cognosdashboards .com, and idashboards.com. Each of these is simple to install and makes beautiful dashboards. The benefit of these is that results are easy to quantify and grasp when viewed as graphics.

with analytics for a fee. Starting with free tools is a good way to go since they help you get the hang of what data is available and how you can grab it and move it to a dashboard or document it. Don't get wedded to the free tools if you outgrow them. If you're working for a large organization or one depending heavily on the success of social campaigns, make sure to check out some of the fee-based information gathering systems.

There's no single, perfect way to display measurements and analytics that make everyone happy. The goal is to track the right elements and graphically display them so that anyone can glean actionable information from the results. If you don't invest resources in learning to use measuring tools and think through what needs to be measured and analyzed, you'll thrash around in the social space and take too long to figure out what works. Time is of the essence because your competitors are trying to figure out how to use these, as well. Rapid pilot projects and experimentation are great, but only if you measure the results and learn your lessons.

SOCIAL INFORMATION SITES

TOOLS We mentioned these sites earlier in the book because they're a great way to get information on your online reputation. They're also helpful in gathering information when you run specific campaigns. Free sites include socialmention.com, twittalyzer, klout, and trendr, for example. If you want to move up and pay for better reporting, try Radian6, Viralheat, and Sm2 (Alterian).

Communicating Measurements to the Team

Once you have your measurement systems in place, think about how you want to use them to inform your team of progress. Nothing inspires people like success, so having sophisticated ways to show people when they're winning is a great tactic for revving them up. Even those who aren't involved with a specific project will be interested in the results because it teaches them what's working in the social space. If you

Providing Analytics for Specific Leaders

TRICKS OF THE TRADE

Once you have professional analytics and measurement systems in place, think about whom you'd like to share them with. It's often a good idea to review them with leaders who are high up in the organization so they can have the information on this critical topic and be aware of the pioneering work your team is doing. This helps your buy-in when you want to test out further use, or when you need budget dollars to buy more professional applications. Also be sure to send the numbers to the executives regularly. By providing analytics monthly you'll keep social tech top of mind with those high up in the organization.

try something and it doesn't work, share that, as well, so everyone knows not to try that specific tactic.

As a general rule, provide high level social statistics monthly and to a wide audience. Campaign-specific measurements and analytics should go out at the end of the program, and should be shared with the entire team, at least. Every time you send out information about the progress or findings on a campaign or pilot project, you'll make people think about social tools and their value. The same has been true for Web site analytics. When we share information on unique visitor growth or the top pages viewed, we're not only telling people "who" information, we're also subtly showing them the importance of the Web site. The fact that managers are taking the time to measure something says a lot about what they value.

Setting Stretch Goals

When you sit down to figure out what goals you'd like to hit for a specific effort, give some thought of how high to set them. It's a truism that you often get what you *expect* to receive. If you set low goals, people will meet them easily—and no one will learn much from the experience. If you set them overly high, people won't even attempt to reach them because they'll feel they're impossible. In other words, there's a real art to setting goals at the best level to both inspire people to reach them and also help everyone learn new skills in the process.

When setting goals in the social space, it's a good idea to set them a bit higher than you normally would. That's because setting high goals forces people to think about how they might achieve them. Because this

> **FOR EXAMPLE**
>
> ### NUMBER OF SUBSCRIBERS
>
> An example of making people think is seen when looking at how Ford has developed Facebook fan pages for all of its car and truck models. By setting a high goal of using social tools to improve sales on each vehicle by measurable amounts, it was forced to develop campaigns for each vehicle individually. This helped Ford lead the automobile industry in the use of Facebook as a marketing tool.

is such a new area, there are lots of creative and innovative ways to accomplish progress. You only bring that out of people if you set goals a little higher than might be comfortable.

As a manager, you're the most responsible person for setting goals, then measuring the dynamics that lead to success. This is the framework that keeps projects on track and helps the team learn best practices for repeating success. Analytics and measurements provide the scorecard you need to know when social tools work and when they need adjustment.

Set your goals high, measure the progress, and analyze the drivers of success. You'll be surprised how quickly you'll be an expert in this new field.

Manager's Checklist for Chapter 10

☑ What gets measured gets done. If managers don't have a process to measure social tech usage and progress, they aren't really managing.

☑ There are many free tools available so there's no excuse for not putting together a management dashboard. Experiment with free sites and learn how well they might perform for your organization. Then move to fee-based services if you're large enough or have a critical need for enterprise-class capabilities.

☑ Analytics need to be done monthly without fail so trends can be monitored regularly in case conditions change. Trending is as important as statistics.

☑ Analytics need to be communicated to a wide audience so that everyone is clear on the progress with social tools, or lack thereof. The more people see the results, the more they can make wise choices when using these tools.

☑ You must use these analytics to hold people accountable for making progress in needed areas. That includes their personal progress in using social tools, and also the progress of organizational campaigns.

☑ You must set stretch goals that help employees really think about how they can use social tools in new and efficient ways to make progress. Set goals too low, and you hinder progress. Set them high, and people try to figure out how to reach them. Be careful not to set unachievable goals because people will lose any hope of reaching them.

Chapter 11

Integrating Social Tech with Velocity

Technology is a set of tools, and in the hands of someone who understands how to use them they can almost appear magical. The past 20 years have been a wonderful time to be a manager in that new technologies have kept us on our toes. We navigated the integration of personal computers and all of their personal productivity tools into our daily skill sets. Then along came the Web and we had to learn to leverage the many benefits it's brought us. The first generation of Web tools were focused on e-commerce and using the Internet as a powerful new way to drive revenue. This Web 1.0 capability completely reordered industries like the travel, classified ads, and music spaces and forever changed how people research new products and vendors. Now we have Web 2.0, aka the social technology era, and we must learn to leverage these awesome tools, as well. And in the same way, social tech will reorder additional industries. Five years from now, we very well may look back and think of the year 2000 as part of the dark ages in communication and connection capabilities.

If you reflect on the last 20 years of technology tool adoption, you'll see a pattern that's important to recognize. The leaders who learn to leverage technology tools faster than those around them (competitors) are the ones who progress. There's little that's positive about being the last one on the block to put a technology to use.

> **THE NEWS INDUSTRY**
>
> **FOR EXAMPLE**
>
> As an example of how a social technology will reorder one industry, we need look no further than the impact of Twitter on the news space. For the first time in history, we have the ability for citizen journalists to publish news in an instant to everyone on Earth with an Internet connection. This has resulted in Twitter being a virtual real-time news source. So much so, that traditional news sources have to monitor Twitter to find breaking stories. As Twitter use widens, many people will look to it as their only news source. Good or bad, citizen journalists are changing news gathering forever.

The only argument against it is that you might avoid some mistakes that the early adopters will make. If you go this route, the question you always have to answer is whether the price you pay by being a late technology adopter is more expensive than the risk of pioneering.

Each of us has a preferred state for the amount of change we're comfortable with, and each person makes ongoing decisions about what tools you'll leverage in your career. We all make conscious choices about the specific pace of new technology adoption we're willing to adopt, and the options will either be:

- **A First Mover.** This is the first organization (person) to pioneer a new product or technique. At times, you might include the first three or four organizations, if they're all taking a slightly different spin on a concept.
- **A Fast Follower.** These are the organizations (people) that learn a few lessons from the first movers, and then act quickly to correct them and launch their own efforts.
- **The Herd.** This refers to the majority of entities that are neither early nor late to the party. They are lukewarm.

> **KEY TERM**
>
> **Fast Follower** Many experts believe that the best place to be on the adoption curve is a fast follower. They postulate that the first movers often pay a heavy price in experimenting with a completely new field, whereas the fast followers avoid the early mistakes but still leverage a new technology fast enough to get the benefit of leveraging the positive aspects before their competition can get up to speed.

- **A Slow Adopter.** These organizations (people) fall into two categories: those who are conservative and purposefully wait until a new technology or model is proven—for sure; or they're just too ignorant to know they're behind. However, they don't hate technology. They're just slow to adopt it.
- **A Luddite.** These are the folks who have a visceral dislike of technology. They don't like progress, and relish doing things the old way. Not because it works, but because they know how to do it that way.

As you look at this list, the important thing to know is that every person and every organization falls somewhere on that list. To prosper in this new knowledge-based economy, you need to consciously choose a strategy of how fast you adopt technology tools, and the best choice is one of the first two options.

> **Luddite** If you think you might be a luddite and aren't aware of this term, we suggest you Google it. Oh, sorry . . . if you're a luddite you don't use Google, do you?
>
> **KEY TERM**

Why Being Early Is a Positive

This should be a simple concept, yet people struggle to understand the value of being early to use a new technology. When budgets are an issue, there can be realities that stop people from being early adopters or fast followers. But when the underlying tools are free (as are most social tech applications), there should be no reason not to at least experiment with implementing something that has possibilities. It's a simple concept: if you can gain value from using a new technology tool over one of the old tools you've used, the faster you can get the technology in play, the sooner you can reap the reward. This is especially true when in a competitive situation because any time you can get a lead on your competition by using a new tool, you'll grab extra benefit until they catch up.

Unfortunately, people are getting burned out on the pace of change in the technology space and are getting jaded about continuously implementing new tools. You have to make good decisions about the added value of using new tools versus the time loss of implementing them. The danger comes when you extend this argument to a whole class of tools

THE MOBILE PHONE MERRY-GO-ROUND The current state of mobile devices is an example of how fast things can change in technology and how difficult it is to decide when to adopt something new. About every 30 days a new "game changing" mobile device is announced. The struggle is making the decision about when to get a new device and accept the learning curve that comes along with it.

and say things like, "We don't have time to invest in social tech, nor do we want our employees playing with it." Given the possibilities of social tech, this is an unenlightened view.

When new technology tools have the potential to make a dramatic difference in team performance, you have a decision to make. Every time you agree to try out a new social tech tool, you know the team has to invest lots of time and energy in learning how to use it, measure it, and prosper with it. Because of this, there's not really an option for you to try every new shiny object that comes along. Yet turning a blind eye to all new social tools could leave you looking for a job when someone above you decides you're standing in the way of progress.

The best thing for the organization is to position yourself as a fast follower of social tech trends, and be careful to understand whom you need to be following. This doesn't mean waiting for all your competitors to implement new uses of social tools. It means keeping a close eye on industries that tend to be leading edge and quickly implementing tools and concepts *in your space* as soon as you see them working in another. In other words, you want to be third or fourth in the overall market to try something new, but first in your industry, if possible.

Here's another reason it's so critical to be early into a market with new technology tools. New concepts in areas like social tech often represent improvements in either an ability to generate new revenues or an ability to lower backoffice costs. In both cases, these results improve profitability. This makes the organization more competitive in the market, and again, the stronger your organization is at achieving its goals when compared to the competition, the more momentum you gained until they catch up.

Not only that, when you use new technology tools and processes, your constituents (customers, partners, vendors, employees, etc.) notice

> ## THE BLEEDING EDGE
>
> **CAUTION**
>
> There's a fine line between being a market leader and the bleeding edge. A smart manager has the discretion to know when a new social tool has been vetted by another organization but has not been applied in his or her market. There's a small window where implementing a new option will provide huge rewards. Adopt it too early, and you'll be the organization that's the bleeding edge example. Adopt it a bit too late, and you'll be seen as copying your competition. There are no points given for this.

that you're a market leader. This reputation translates into a positive perception of your brand as an innovator, and people generally love innovators. People also want to do business with a clear market leader because they believe success breeds success. Who wouldn't want to partner with Google, Microsoft, Nike, Proctor & Gamble, or General Electric?

The Impact on Your Career

For you personally, there's a great opportunity in developing a visionary eye for new social tech concepts. There's also great danger if you operate at either extreme of the continuum. If you're constantly pushing the envelope with the latest new toy, your bosses will lose respect for your management decision capabilities. If you have to be forced into trying every new social concept after everyone else in the organization is using it, you'll be having a difficult conversation with your boss one day.

The most important decision you can make *today* is where you're going to be on this continuum. You can't go on without making a conscious choice or you'll end up in the wrong place. For some, you might have to set aside your personal preference and make a decision that's best for the organization.

Over the next five years, your ability to grasp social tech tools and apply them quickly will make a big difference in how those around you view your performance. Much like Internet skills ten years ago, social tech skills will become a requirement. This means they won't be optional, so it's better to pick your pace of adoption and learn how to experiment and implement these tools and concepts quickly. Whatever you're responsible for in the organization, there are ways you can use something under the social umbrella to improve performance.

SMART MANAGING
THE IMPACT OF AGE

Let's generalize for a moment. The longer you've been a manager, the harder it will be for you to willingly change your ways of operating. In other words, the harder it will be for you to evangelize the use of social tools on your team. Keep this in mind when you decide what your speed of adoption should be for the organization. You may be a fast adopter in a conservative company and you need to tone it down. You may be a slow adopter in a fast-changing market and you'll have to speed things up. The best pace may not be what you want personally, but what your team needs to succeed.

To gain value from trying out a new social tool, you must shorten the time between the initial experiment and the implementation. You either want to find out quickly how something can be of value, or you want to move on before it wastes too many resources. To do this well, you need a model for quickly trying out and testing new social techniques.

MISTAKE PROOFING
I DON'T WANT TO BE FIRST!

Be careful to base your decisions on leveraging social tools on how your specific group can use them. Some of you may not want to be the first manager in the organization to push the envelope with social tools. Don't let this fear hold you back. If you run the accounting department and think you can use social tools, then use them, regardless of any past history of waiting until other groups pioneer the use of technologies.

Pilot Projects as a Velocity Tool

In the Goals, Measurements, and Analytics chapter, we talked about pilot projects and the need to analyze the results. The reason we want you to understand the pilot project model is because it creates velocity in taking an idea from a thought to a full-fledged new tactic in your strategy. In some cases, piloting new concepts will quickly demonstrate that an idea was not the winner you thought it was. That's OK; no one is perfect. You don't need every experiment to work perfectly to get to a valuable find.

By the way, we're not proposing that every time you want to try out a social tool that you run a full-out pilot project. There are some basic social concepts that only require having one of your people test out a new tool for a few days and report whether he or she liked it. Apply the pilot project

> ## A New Social Sales Model
> An example of a social concept that would require a pilot proj-
> ect would be implementation of an eWord of mouth viral
> advertising campaign as a replacement of some form of tradi-
> tional advertising. Instead of dropping your current form of advertising
> all at once and shifting 100 percent of resources to a social advertising
> model, develop a pilot project that can measure precisely the ROI of an e-
> Word of mouth campaign versus your current advertising model.

concept when you're going to invest a serious amount of resources to test out a concept that could have dramatic results for the organization.

When you're sure a pilot project is needed, it's important to be scientific about how the pilot is configured and analyzed. We used the term *scientific* multiple times in the earlier chapter because we wanted to make it clear that numbers can give you great insight, but only if you're careful how you structure what you're analyzing. The same is true with pilot projects. Each one should be set up to help you learn specific things about the particular social method you're testing. The point of a pilot project is not to throw something on the wall and see if it sticks. It's to experiment in such a way that you can discern the drivers that could make the new concept valuable or the hurdles that stop it from being of value.

Whether you call it a pilot project, market testing, campaign analysis, or experimentation, you've been doing this for years. Every food company of any size tests new flavors and packaging on a small, regional basis before it commits to running the worldwide release of a new product. Using an organized test in the small market limits risk and produces important information about how to successfully do a full roll-out.

The Pilot Project Process

There are many ways you can configure a pilot process to test a concept. We're not trying to give you the definitive story on everything you could do, just a simple model that will work for most of your social tech experiments. The most important thing to know is that you must be organized, document the intentions, and frame what you're going to do and what you want to learn. Here are the minimum elements that must be documented and why they're important:

- **The name of the project.** This is the common vocabulary that you'll use to identify the effort. The name can be important because it might identify the result expected so people are clear on what you're playing for. For example, you could name a pilot "The Twitter Project" or you could call it "The Revenue on Demand Project." These names will have a different feel within the organization.

- **Who owns the responsibility for the project.** This is the person or persons who'll be held accountable for execution of the project. They normally own the responsibility to make sure all tasks get done and that measurements are gathered and distributed. They also do the reporting when meetings are held to review progress.

- **The timeframe for the entire project.** This includes the start date, the end date, and the milestones in between, if any. The duration of a pilot project must be considered. Not allowing enough time could create an unnecessary failure. Allowing a pilot to run too long may delay taking the lessons learned and turning them into standard practices that the organization could benefit from.

- **The project's goals.** These are the metrics you hope to accomplish. These should be measurable for the most part. For example, getting 10,000 people to follow a blog is a measurable goal. Learning to write a blog is a goal, but difficult to measure. Generally, you want to define goals you'd like to accomplish, which, if achieved, would show from a numbers standpoint the pilot was a success. Remember, even if you give it your best shot and miss your targets, you learn from the experience and know what not to do next time.

- **The description of the pilot.** This is a narrative description that details how the pilot project is going to work. It should cover what tools are going to be used, who is going to be targeted, and why you're doing the pilot project.

- **What is to be learned from doing the pilot.** This may be the most important element and needs to be well thought out. It's a list of the specific concepts you want to learn about within the pilot. They're the elements you need to be able to do well. The first step is to learn if you can do them at all. The second step is to find out the best practices for getting them done.

LEARNING LESSONS QUICKLY

SMART

MANAGING

One of the most important ways to use a pilot project is to have a clear understanding of what you want to learn from doing them. There are almost always at least three things that can be learned from every pilot, and only by clearly identifying and measuring them can you gain the benefit of understanding. For example, a pilot project to learn how to save money through using crowdsourcing as a market research tool might be divided into the following pieces: (1) learn how to get a large number of people to participate and share opinions; (2) learn what the top five product ideas are from the crowd; (3) learn what software features are most needed when leveraging the crowd to get their opinions.

■ **How will success be measured.** This final element specifies exactly how the pilot project's value will be measured. Success could be in achieving the goals. Success could also be in simply learning the lessons we set out to learn. It could even be in learning how to run a pilot well, and teaching the pilot owners how to run the process.

We suggest you create your own syllabus shell document that outlines the elements you want to document for your pilot projects. This gives you an easy way to hand a blank form to anyone who's going to own a project so he or she can have a "fill-in-the-blanks" place to start. If you would like to download our basic pilot project shell, go to the resources section of our Web site at enterprisesocialtechnology.com.

Building a Culture of Velocity

It bears asserting that if you want your team to adopt social tools quickly and be good at running rapid pilot projects, you must develop a culture of velocity. Groups of humans typically develop a cultural proclivity to either move quickly or be judiciously slow. These variances in culture are obvious if we look at examples like Apple, Google, and Hollywood, versus churches, schools, and the government. Your team falls somewhere along this scale, and you're partly responsible for whatever speed they exhibit.

Within the larger framework of the organization's cultural speed of adoption, your team will look to you as a model. If they see you value early adoption and experimentation, they'll feel they need to do this, as

A Slow High Performer

What do you do with a high performer who routinely speaks negatively about using new tools or moving forward at the pace you require? Allowing the person to do his or her own thing is a dangerous mistake. This sends a message to the others you have different expectations for "special" people. It's important that even reluctant high performers understand that they can benefit from using new social tools, and the faster they can put them to use the more they'll assure that they stay performing at a high level.

well. At the same time, your willingness to hold people accountable for moving quickly to learn new social concepts will have an impact. We mentioned earlier the possibility of adding goals to employee reviews around the use of social tools. This is a great example of how you can institutionalize an effort to create velocity.

Once you can establish a team culture where the peers influence each other to move quickly and be adaptive, you'll find that new people will look around and see what's expected. This dynamic only gets created if you make a conscious effort to get your team to a place where they *all* are willing to adopt new technologies, or at least give them a try.

You can be a visionary or an early adopter and have the best intentions as a manager, but if you don't nurture a culture of velocity within your team, you'll simply be a voice telling them to go left, while they're constantly going right.

The Problems with Size

It's only fair to acknowledge that the velocity at which a team gravitates toward new social tools has a lot to do with the size of the organization. The smaller you are, the easier it is to test things and be innovative. There are fewer inhibitors to downloading a new application and giving it a go or experimenting with a new concept like crowdsourcing by going to a site and posting a bounty to get a task done.

The larger you are, the more rules, procedures, and bureaucracy you face and that can limit velocity. If you want to do the same crowdsourcing test you'd have to get two approvals and then find a way to use a company credit card on the site. This is simply a necessary evil for larger organizations so things don't get out of control. On the other hand, if you're a manager within a large firm, it can be frustrating to get pilot projects approved, resources for new tools, and approval to experiment with new methods.

For this reason, you must play a different role in creating velocity if you work for a large entity. Not only do you have to

THE LARGER YOU ARE, THE MORE YOU BLOCK

FOR EXAMPLE

An example of what slows velocity within a larger organization is that the larger you are, the higher the probability that social tech usage is blocked. Very few firms with less than 20 employees block usage, whereas more than 50 percent of large organizations block usage in some form.

inspire your team to move quickly, you also have to play a politician's role with those above you so that the road is cleared to do pilot projects and test new social tools. The benefit to being at a large organization is that if you figure out how to apply social tools, you may end up being a shining light with your results getting shared across the organization, and that can only be good for your career.

Small organizations have the luxury of moving quickly since they're unfettered by rules and guidelines, and the only danger you have to watch for is being overly distracted by launching too many efforts. You're the leader, so if you're lucky enough to have free reign as a manager, be sure you're not chasing every rabbit that runs past.

Case Studies for Velocity

This discussion of speed is more than just theory. There are many examples of companies prospering through early adoption of social tools, and many managers who have become stars because they were willing to make the time investment to learn how to use social tools before other people in the organization.

JetBlue is a successful up-and-comer in the airline space, and that's saying something because flying people around the world has been a tough business lately. One reason JetBlue is winning is its culture of leveraging new concepts and ideas faster than its competitors. This was certainly true when it came to using Twitter as a tool. As of this writing, JetBlue has nearly two million followers and its rate of adding followers is still climbing.

JetBlue's closest competitor is Southwest Airlines, and it has less than half that number. JetBlue has pioneered the use of Twitter as a sales channel and has successfully built a model where the company can provide instant discounts on flights that have seats to fill. The fact that they've figured out this model before their competitors is helping them gain revenue and new customers they simply wouldn't have had without their culture of velocity.

Jeff Hurt was formerly the manager in charge of events for the National Association of Dental Plans until his recent move to Velvet Chainsaw, a consulting firm. A large part of this change in career happened because Jeff was an early adopter of social tools. Three years ago he heard a presentation that included a description of a new crop of social tech tools. He made it a personal mission to learn how to use these tools and to connect with as many people as possible. Over the next two years he raised his career profile to such a degree that he became well known across the country in his space. His early adoption of social tech and the example he set for the people around him led to a beneficial career move.

We're not suggesting that speed in and of itself is always the answer. We're also not saying that you need to always be the first one to use a social tool. What we are saying is that when tools prove themselves to be valuable, you must move with velocity to leverage the benefits. Because you're a manager, you're also a leader, and this means that you set the pace of adoption. Take a moment to consider whether your personal pace of adoption is at odds with your organization's.

If you're naturally ahead of your employer, think about becoming an evangelist and helping the larger team benefit from what you see and learn. If you're naturally a slower adopter than your employer, make a decision today to invest time and energy in this new field so that you at least don't injure your career.

Manager's Checklist for Chapter 11

☑ To win with social tools, you must learn to identify those that will be the most valuable to your organization and get them implemented quickly. It's especially important to do this faster than your competition.

☑ You must apply an organized process for experimenting with tools and concepts that have potential to learn what value may be there to reap.

☑ The framework and elements you choose for your pilot process must be documented. Each pilot project must be organized, owned by someone, measured, and analyzed to get the value from the test.

☑ The most important element of a pilot project is to identify the exact things that you want to learn from running the effort. There will normally be at least three different dynamics that can be learned and you need to be clear on what they are.

☑ The world is speeding up, so you have to be able to move quickly to identify valuable social tools. There's an advantage to applying these tools before your competition and reaping the value before they can catch up. In addition, you'll get a reputation from your customers as being a thought leader, and that is a good thing.

☑ If your organization is large and you have lots of rules and regulations, it will be your job to negotiate these hurdles so your team can get the benefit of social tools. Don't wait to be told by the home office what to do with them.

Chapter

12

The Future of Managing Social Tech

One of the most critical roles a manager has is to be the person who guides the team toward a future vision of success. You simply cannot focus solely on executing today's game plan without giving some consideration to what the future playing field might look like. The ability to predict what will happen over the next few years so that you can help your team have the best shot at succeeding is the essence of leadership. Without a picture in your head of what will happen in the coming years, you have no way of making solid decisions today that will be beneficial tomorrow. You can't merely oversee daily activities; you must also be constantly planning for the changes that are sure to come.

This plays out in the reality of setting budgets, hiring and terminating employees, training people for future needs, providing expansion capabilities for office space, and being aware of the latest tools that can help reach the organization's goals. These tasks require you to have a clear picture of where your organization and industry will move tomorrow.

When it comes to social technologies, looking ahead becomes a must because technology tools can be fads that cool off after too much hype (e.g., Second Life). Or at other times, they climb slowly into full usage by everyone (e-mail). Still others will explode onto the scene and climb rapidly to millions and millions of users (Facebook and Twitter). You need a way to gauge

SMART

MANAGING

LOOKING AHEAD

A critical area of discernment for a manager is to know how far into the future to strategize. This depends on the environment you work in. A manager at a department of transportation must look years and years into the future to understand what traffic patterns will be like. A manager at a hospital might be concerned about what the health-care space will be like in 18 months. The important task here is to consider carefully how far you personally should be looking ahead.

what's going to be an accepted tool. Otherwise, you'll be whipsawed between concerns over the risk of putting effort into things that don't work or waiting too long on social tools that become standard.

For this reason, you must consider flexing your visionary wings when making decisions on adopting new social tools or running pilot projects. Your skill at predicting what you should implement and experiment with today versus leave off the list could seriously impact how you're viewed by your boss. Employees with an accurate vision of the future make decisions that lead organizations to success. People without the ability to look forward make poor decisions on implementing new tools, and that's never helpful to your career.

Making Good Decisions Today

We all want to make good decisions, and we all want to look good. If we could accurately predict the future, we would all make good decisions. Still, there are people who see the future staring them in the face and don't get it. It's often this way with social tech. There are very clear indications of where this is all headed. We know organizations will all have a voice through some kind of channel (Facebook, Twitter, blogs, etc.). We know people and organizations will have online reputations. We know crowdsourcing will be a powerful way to get things done. We also know young generations are adopting these tools in droves so if nothing else, as they get into the workforce, they'll bring them along. Yet many older people still sit on the sidelines and refuse to put any energy into understanding these new dynamics.

The first step in making good decisions today is to recognize that the common use of social tools is still being accomplished by early adopters and will steadily go mainstream over the next few years. In other words, don't fight it. When you're faced with decisions of whether to allow social tech use at the office, what tools to standardize on, or whether to experiment with some new application of social usage, know that holding back the tide or being timid isn't going to serve you.

The next step to making good decisions with social tools today is to do your own

OBSERVING GEN Y

FOR EXAMPLE

It's clear that people younger than 25 years old operate differently from their elders. If you want a quick glimpse into the future, you need only look at the fact that about 95 percent of this age group uses social tools. They have no fear of experimenting with new tools and have little history of working any other way. They also have an expectation that when a social tool makes sense to them, everyone else should adopt it.

homework. You must get *personally* knowledgeable about how these tools work, why they get popular, how they can generate value for the organization, and when there's a better version to move to. You can't delegate this entire field to someone else. You can get help from others on the fringes, but you shouldn't opt out of personally using the tools because you're frustrated with having to learn something new. You must have first-hand knowledge of these tools to have the information clearly

RUBBER-STAMPING

CAUTION

It's seductive to pull together a few twenty-somethings and ask them for their opinions on social tech, then make decisions based on this. Research is valuable, but you can't outsource important management decisions to others simply because you're too lazy to learn about the tools yourself.

in front of you to make good future decisions.

The final step in good decision making is to always look at your decisions through a lens of what they will mean in a few years. For example, it might be a real pain today to do lots of training with your sales force on social tools. They need to be out selling and they need to stay focused.

If you only look at today, why invest time in teaching them concepts like *socially facilitated selling*? However, when viewed through a lens of what they will need to close deals two years from now, it's clear they'll need to add social tech skills to their bag.

Socially Facilitated Selling
KEY TERM Refers to a new selling model where a number of social tools and concepts are leveraged to create an environment that makes it easier to close deals. It also includes teaching the salespeople a package of social tech skills to give them an advantage in the marketplace.

Being short-sighted about anything will not be good for your career. Being short-sighted about adopting social technologies will teach you that lesson in a negative way if you allow it, which leads us to the next subject.

How Embracing Social Tech Can Lift Your Career

The purpose of this book is to give you knowledge and tools to help you move forward in your career and to benefit the organization. Be clear what you're playing for, because integrating social tech into your day isn't just about doing what's popular or cool this quarter, it's about learning to use a powerful set of new tools and techniques that can change the game.

There seem to be three kinds of managers at this point in the social adoption curve: the thought leaders, the dragged along, and the naysayers. Two of these aren't helping themselves, or anyone else for that matter. Somewhere between being a thought leader and being dragged along is a place where a manager is quick to adopt new methods of doing things, but not on the bleeding edge. This is where most of you should be. If you feel you're behind, you probably are. If you feel you're too old to learn new tricks, you probably are. If you feel you're too busy to invest any time in this field, you have your priorities out of whack. Or, you could choose to suck it up and embrace social technologies for what they are—a powerful new set of tools.

Personal Use

There are two critical ways to apply social tool skills. The first is in how you use the tools in your daily routine, and the second is how you implement the tools with your team. With everything you've read to this point, it should be easy to see how each of the bullet points below can be yours if you're willing to invest the time. This lists the direct benefits of leveraging social tech on a personal level:

- **A much-improved network of contacts.** No matter what you do for a living, there's value in having a robust network of people you can reach out to when you need to get something done. Social tools allow you to keep hundreds of contacts fresh, as opposed to the past, when keeping even 30 or 40 up to date was a chore.

■ **A better river of information.** You can build your own continuous learning process, and done right, this translates into a high career IQ.

■ **An ability to become a recognized expert online.** Social tools give you a new ability to share your unique expertise online. You have the potential to invest a little time each day, sharing the observations, ideas, and resources you discover so others can benefit. This leads to an active and large list of people who want to follow what you say, and that translates into being a recognized expert. In many ways, this can help your career.

■ **The improved ability to manage remote workers.** There are unique dynamics for managing remote workers well. Social tools give you the ability to communicate in better ways than strictly over the phone or e-mail. They also facilitate collaboration and improve communication among team members.

■ **The creation and nurturing of a stellar online reputation.** With every day, it is more commonplace for people to search online to learn about you. Most people would be shocked if they could see in real time who and how many people search for information on them. This includes people you'd like to do business with, sell to, hire, or influence. What they find online will have a huge impact on how they'll relate to you going forward.

■ **A reputation within your organization as a leader with skills and vision.** When people around you evaluate your performance as a manager, they take into account many things. One of the skills that's

---

SHOW DON'T TELL

TRICKS OF THE TRADE

If you really want to impress those around and above you, make sure you show them you understand social tech by using it. This is a tool that's better demonstrated than simply explained because just talking a good game won't impress people. For example, don't just tell people about the concept of crowdsourcing. Go out and find a task you're doing in-house and crowdsource it. Then measure the ROI and tell people all about your amazing results.

growing in importance is your ability to use technology tools. You could be the greatest people person in the firm and if you can't use a computer, people will rate you as average overall. You must have the whole package. If you'll employ the concepts and ideas you've read in this book, the people around you will be impressed with your skills and forward thinking.

Some managers make lots of excuses to themselves about why they're not jumping into the social tech world. They claim to be too busy, too set in their ways, or too far behind to catch up. The only way you can justify these things to yourself is if you completely ignore what the future workplace will be like. For your own sake, be willing to invest in yourself even if you'll only be managing for a few more years. And if you're really not worried about your career, how about being willing to invest in your team?

Team Use

When it comes to the value you can create by teaching social tech tools and concepts to your team, you'll be surprised at the overall uplift in performance. If you choose to apply your newfound skills to assist people with implementing social tools in their careers, each one could perform at a higher level, and when added together, the results can be dramatic. For motivation, you need only hold in your head a picture of what your team could be doing in the future, if they invested a little time and energy today.

Here are a few of the benefits investment in your team could bring:

- **A higher level of communication among team members.** Social tools provide new ways to communicate internally. This is especially true if your team is dispersed. Lack of communication is often cited as one the biggest factors in a failed project or effort. Opening up communication channels (Yammer, Twitter, collaboration tools, Facebook, online discussion groups, shared knowledge-bases, etc.) so that your team has real-time, efficient, and easy ways to keep each other informed would improve performance in ways you can't imagine today.

- **A better river of information.** When you help your team develop deeper and real-time flows of information into their brains, you'll raise the collective IQ. More knowledge leads to better decisions. Better decisions lead to higher productivity and better profit percentages. Have we mentioned that knowledge is power?

> **RIVER SOURCES**
>
> **TRICKS OF THE TRADE**
>
> A best practice you can do with your team is to periodically have people share what their favorite new sources of information are with the rest of the team. Make this a regular part of your staff meetings by setting aside a few minutes at the beginning of the meeting for people to explain what information they've discovered lately and how they are using it. This both forces people to always be looking for something they can share with others, and keeps everyone's rivers of information fresh.

- **A happier, more productive workplace.** *Harvard Business Review* published an article that showed the use of social tools produced a happier and more productive workforce. This is especially the case for workers under 30 years old. When organizations ban social usage, they cut off many knowledge workers from a critical piece of their source of knowledge. There will always be someone who abuses this privilege but that's not a good enough reason to ban usage by everyone. If it were, all companies would ban phone usage, as well.

- **A better ability to tap into knowledge and human resources.** With a robust ability to use social tools, employees will tap these channels to get help from their contacts and answers from people who specialize in the solutions to their problems. Social technologies tap the collective and the collective is a powerful knowledge source. This is the reason game shows allow contestants to poll the audience when they need help, and the collective audience never seems to be wrong.

- **Additional options for getting projects completed on time and on budget.** If you manage in a world where projects must get done, social tools give you some strong options. Crowdsourcing can give you access to new vendors and less expensive and faster ways to get things done. Online collaboration software helps team members move through the project with greater velocity because they have better visibility into what other team members are doing. If team members on a project are dispersed, the new communication options under the social umbrella can help people stay in touch seamlessly.

Your team is going head to head with teams at every competing organization. Why would you cripple your team by failing to give them access and knowledge about tools and techniques that will help them win? This sounds obvious, yet every day most managers are allowing this to happen. Hopefully you aren't one of them!

If you want to light up your team, provide access to social tools they're not aware of. Going even further, you share a vision of the future with them so they see what their workplace will be like in the coming years. This kind of investment in your team is what makes you a manager who is respected throughout your people's careers. If you'd love to paint this picture but are struggling with where all of this may go, here are some ideas you can use.

What Are the Next Big Things in Social Tech?

There's no need to consult a crystal ball when trying to look into the future. We can extrapolate from current trends and predictions about some of the twists and turns that will likely be coming. It really isn't that difficult to figure out *what* will happen in the future, it's just tough to know exactly *when* it will go mainstream. Everything on the list below will surely come to pass. The question is whether it will happen in one year or three:

- **Standardization of social tools.** Standards are lacking in the social space at the moment. This causes us to waste time on tasks like having to enter new passwords on sites over and over. We have to connect with friends and contacts on every new site we sign up with. When we write mobile applications, we have to create versions for multiple operating systems. The list goes on. As this field matures, we'll have organizations that will suggest and promote standards that when accepted, will make using new tools much easier.
- **Portable profiles.** We currently have to enter profile photos and information with every site we sign up for. Soon we'll have a way to create one profile and supply it to all sites we want to use. This eases the maintenance issues of updating multiple sites when something changes, and will make it easier to belong to multiple eCommunities.
- **Virtual worlds provide a 3D interface to the Web.** Don't let the fact that

Second Life was overhyped fool you. Virtual worlds and the virtual meeting spaces that go along with them will be back with a vengeance. We'll one day turn the entire Web into a 3D environment instead of the 2D world it is now. As bandwidth gets more plentiful and 3D graphic technology gets more realistic, we'll see a resurgence of virtual world tools.

- **Crowdsourcing explodes in volume of use.** There are billions of people in the world who will become Internet-enabled over the next five years. As they do, they'll be able to make more money over the Web than they can in their local neighborhood. They will flock to crowdsourcing sites where they'll bid on work and perfect the art of making money in the knowledge economy. Crowdsourcing will generate 100 times the volume of work that outsourcing does today.

- **People-rating sites grow quickly and have serious impact.** We're very close to having people-rating Web sites where all of us will be listed and people will have the ability to rate us. This capability really does not exist today at scale, but it will very soon. When this happens, it will radically change how we learn about each other and the impressions we form at the beginning of relationships. We mentioned Honestly.com earlier. Look for sites like this one to create a new capability we've never had before—the ability to review an honest assessment of a person by those they have encountered in the past.

- **Immersive and filtered, real-time rivers of information.** We're overwhelmed today with the vast river of information that the Web and social tools bring us. The answer won't be to turn off the spigot, it will be to learn to filter and ingest information faster and easier. This will take lots of new forms as we search for better ways to get exactly the information we need, where we need it, and when we need it. In addition, we'll develop sophisticated ways to build alerts that fill us in immediately with critical information, and then organize the rest into categories that we can access at will. Having a powerful river of information won't be optional, and skills in setting these up will be looked at as a serious differentiator.

- **Communication profiles assist with contacts.** One of the biggest holes in our ability to communicate with each other is that no one provides a central profile of our methods for connecting. Sure, most of us have a cell phone, e-mail, and a LinkedIn address; many more have Twitter, Facebook, Foursquare, etc. Our mobile devices allow us to text and do video calls with each other. It's wonderful to have all of these ways to communicate, but for the most part, we don't know what people's preferred methods are, what their current status is, or where they are physically. That will change soon because one of the major players will provide this type of profile. Then we'll be able to look a person up, see what tools they use to connect, their preferences, and their status at that moment. Armed with this information, you'll better know how to get in touch with someone.

- **Game theory moving into the business world.** Young people are very attuned to the methods that game providers use to make games challenging and intriguing. The average youth spends 10,000 hours playing games before the age of 18. There are a number of people experimenting with building games that harness the collective thinking and skills of the player base to solve difficult real-world problems. The next step will be to configure business processes so that they're more consistent with how game environments work. In that way you can harness the already-ingrained concepts of the next generation.

- **Pay per mention becomes common.** With online reputations and e-word of mouth becoming more critical to success, we'll see an expanding list of ways to give incentives to people to say positive things about a person or entity. Whether it's giving incentives to bloggers, twitterers, or Facebook powerhouses, the will to control your own public relations will drive this. Add to this the coming people-rating sites, and we'll see an explosion of methods for rewarding people for positive reviews.

At the same time, we'll see an explosion of people who learn the power of the negative comment, and they'll use it whenever they feel wronged. It will take years for us to sort out which comments are legitimate from those that are "sponsored" or coming from bitter people. We already have Web sites that facilitate people creating video advertisements and getting paid to send them to friends. Look for years of sorting out how we feel about being paid to leverage our networks as a sales channel.

TRAINING CONCEPTS

Game theory commonly starts players off at a sandbox level where they can play with the tools and processes of the game and learn how to control elements they'll need to succeed. This level may not even be part of the real game and may be a safe environment for them to learn. Once they progress to level one, they're faced with a challenge so difficult that it seems overwhelming at first. As they play that level over and over, at some point they learn how to win consistently and as soon as they do, they're moved up to a new level and the routine starts all over again. If the player isn't challenged over and over, they get bored and play something else. As a manager, think about the wisdom of taking the same approach with training and motivating your young employees.

We're in the very early days of using the many concepts that come under the umbrella of social technologies. People generally have a hard time extrapolating forward the seeds of innovation that are already planted. We often can barely accept the leading edge uses of technology already available, much less get our arms around what's to come. These dynamics must be overcome if you're to be a powerful manager.

You have a rare opportunity to leverage an explosion of new tools to benefit your career and your organization. These moments in history don't come around that often. We've had two previously with the advent of the personal computer and then the Web (Web sites and e-commerce). You're now in the middle of the next wave of opportunity. You have a choice: either invest time and energy to exploit this opportunity, or get run over by others who will.

Manager's Checklist for Chapter 12

☑ You must use an accurate future view to make good decisions today that will dovetail successfully into that future view.

☑ It's critical that you be able to look into the future and make accurate assumptions about where things will go. As a leader of people, this is a critical piece of what you're uniquely tasked with.

☑ The ability to look into the future accurately isn't magic; it's a process of extrapolating forward trends that are already here.

☑ You are responsible for helping your team see an accurate picture of the future. They're busy with today's tasks and you can influence them through teaching them social tool usage that will benefit the team for years to come.

☑ Learning to be an expert at applying social tools will positively impact your career in many ways, including higher performance levels.

☑ Social technology as a toolset is just in its infancy. Learning to leverage it now will set you up for progress tomorrow.

Index

About the Author

One of the early pioneers with using the Web as a tool, Scott Klososky has been building software companies, and helping clients apply technology since the days when a Web site was a single page. As the Web migrated e-commerce as its hottest use into what's known as Web 2.0, Scott has been on the forefront of speaking and consulting on how organizations can leverage social technologies. He is a well-regarded and sought-after speaker on explaining and implementing social technololgy applications and concepts before they become popular. For this reason, he is invited by organizations again and again to share with people what will be coming next.

In the area of social technology, Scott was one of the first experts to develop a holistic methodology for implementing social tools across an organization. He has also field-tested unique ways to implement new-enterprise social concepts, such as *organizational voice, rivers of information, online reputation management,* and *crowdsourcing.* Connect to Scott through his Web site at **www.klososky.com**, his blog at **www.tech nologystory.com**, and through his many social media channels on sites like YouTube, SlideShare, Scribd, and Google Knol.